Darlings Will, Ka~~~~~~ ~s,

Now you can read all about your
'Robinson Crusoe' great, great, great Uncle!

# The Life of
# Edwin Dodgson

All my love,

Mum,

Caroline,

Gaggy xx

Dec 2020

# The Life of
# Edwin Dodgson

*Brother of Lewis Carroll and Missionary to
the South Atlantic Islands*

BY

EDWARD WAKELING

AND

CAROLINE LUKE

THE CHOIR PRESS

First published in the United Kingdom in 2020 by
The Choir Press

ISBN 978-1-78963-147-0

British Library Cataloguing in Publication Data
The Life of Edwin Dodgson
Dodgson, Edwin Heron – Biography
English – 19th century
Wakeling, Edward
Luke, Caroline

*Dedicated to the memory of*
*Amy Irene Hume Jaques (née Dodgson)*
*1884–1980*

# Contents

———————

# List of Illustrations

———

Photographs taken by Edwin's brother, Rev. C L Dodgson, otherwise known as Lewis Carroll, are listed in Edward Wakeling's *The Photographs of Lewis Carroll: A Catalogue Raisonné* under the given image number (IN). *The Photographs of Lewis Carroll* was published by the University of Texas Press in 2015 (ISBN: 978-0-292-76743-0).

Every effort has been made to locate original copyright holders. Should any still exist, please make contact with the authors so credit may be given in any future edition.

# Introduction

*by Caroline Luke, Great-Great-Niece of Edwin Dodgson*

My fascination with Edwin Dodgson and the island of Tristan da Cunha – often referred to as 'the loneliest island in the world' – began as a child, on visits to my grandmother. She was the eldest daughter of Skeffington, Charles Dodgson's younger brother, and would hold us spellbound with amusing stories, observations and tales of extraordinary people and events. Looking back, she had obviously inherited the Dodgson gene which enabled her to be such a wonderful storyteller.

Many of the tales would revolve around the family, and Uncle Edwin's story was one we found particularly interesting. Edwin, the youngest of the Dodgson family, had sailed to the other side of the world to become the priest and schoolmaster on the isolated island of Tristan da Cunha, home to around one hundred inhabitants. We learnt how, having finally landed on the island, he watched with utter dismay as the ship that had brought him ended up on the rocks and virtually all his precious possessions which were to support him in his role were smashed to pieces in the waves. He became in our imaginations a family Robinson Crusoe. We also learnt of the fulfilments and challenges of his role as the island's priest, his work to establish a school and his attempts to improve the living conditions for the islanders. I was inspired by the bravery and conviction that Edwin – and many other missionaries at that time – had shown in volunteering for such a challenging way of life.

It wasn't until many years later, and after my grandmother had died, that my aunt – who had always lived with my grandmother – passed me a box for safekeeping which she explained contained items 'all about Edwin's time on Tristan da Cunha'. In it I found letters, newspaper cuttings, booklets etc. telling the story of Edwin, his missionary postings and the challenges he faced whilst away in very remote places.

Remembering the stories my grandmother had related, it was wonderful to now be able to read the recollections of the man himself. At a time when relatively few individuals had experienced any form of long-distance travel, his letters provided fascinating descriptions of exotic places, animals, birds, people and local customs for his family back home. In a historical context it is also interesting to note his references to particular hymns of that time, books, magazines and even medicinal treatments.

However, his writing, at times, also gave voice to the worrying episodes of ill health and the desperate loneliness that he felt, often when he received no communication for a long period. In times such as these his faith would be his saviour. He had been brought up in a fervently religious family; his father and two of his older brothers had entered the Church (although Charles did not make it his career), and his father had always encouraged Edwin to follow in his footsteps. Edwin's faith was the main focus for his life.

Having lost his mother at the age of four, Edwin had been cared for by his father, his aunt and seven sisters. They, along with his three older brothers, were a very close family, providing much of their own education and entertainment. He would have grown up enjoying discussions within the family on books, religion, history, inventions and politics. There was also a shared sense of humour, love of imaginative whimsy and fascination for mathematical riddles and puzzles. My grandmother's memory of Edwin in his latter years, when she was staying at the family home of 'the Chestnuts' in Guildford, was that he was blessed with a good sense of humour.

Being so far from home on his various postings meant that communication with the family was of paramount importance. He would eagerly await news of the family, books they were reading and what was happening in the country as a whole. However, communication, particularly when he was on Tristan da Cunha, depended on letters being written, sent to a forwarding address and transported on a ship that may, or may not, then be able to land. This often meant a period of well over a year before he received replies – and of course, sometimes, there might be a delivery of many letters and parcels all at once! This must have been frustrating in the extreme, and it is no surprise that his spirits were, at times, so affected by this. The feeling of isolation and being so distant from what was happening at home must have been very difficult for him.

Although he was given a warm welcome by the people of Tristan and became an integral member of the community, it was a very different lifestyle to the one he was used to at home. Gradually, as more and more problems appeared – rats damaging the crops, insects destroying the roofs – and as he continued to try to educate people with a deeper spiritual awareness, he began to wonder if a collective move to a less remote location might be in everyone's best interests. He enlisted the help of Charles back home, and considerable efforts were made to bring this about. However, he seems not to have recognised the determination of many of the islanders to remain on Tristan no matter what hardships they faced; after all, they had invested a great deal of effort in making it their home. In this context it is perhaps instructive to note that, following a volcanic eruption and full-scale evacuation to the UK in 1961, many islanders made the decision to return home in preference to what they perceived as the pressures of living in a so-called 'civilised society'. Today there is a thriving and sustainable community of over 250 people.

I believe the time has come to set out the story of Edwin and his efforts, as a missionary, to improve the lives of others. His work certainly became his 'calling' and, although he had his struggles and wasn't always able to bring about what, to his mind, was the right way forward, he did indeed play his part in making a difference to the people and the communities where he worked.

The importance of Tristan da Cunha in Edwin's life is well documented herein, and his interest in the island was reciprocated by his family. Perhaps the most recent example of this was during the evacuation in 1961. When news of the impending evacuation reached my grandmother, it prompted her to suggest that, as a family, we should offer accommodation to some of the islanders. In the event, the management of the situation by those responsible forestalled the need for this and it was acknowledged that it would be more beneficial for the Tristanians to be accommodated together in one place.

My contribution to what follows has been very meagre and this project would never have reached fruition if it had not been for the part played by Edward Wakeling, to whom I am greatly indebted. He has carried out meticulous research and, in his usual scholarly fashion, has put into order all the various letters, photographs, editorial notes and written text, which we hope you will enjoy and which will provide a true picture of the Rev. Edwin Dodgson.

# Early Life

Edwin Heron Dodgson (1846–1918) was the youngest of eleven children and the only one among his family to be born at Croft-on-Tees, on the Yorkshire/Durham border. The rest of his siblings were born at Daresbury, Cheshire, including his older brother Charles Lutwidge Dodgson (1832–1898), better known by his famous pseudonym 'Lewis Carroll'. His father, Charles Dodgson (1800–1868), was rector of Croft at the time of Edwin's birth, and later became canon of Ripon and archdeacon of Richmond. His mother was Frances 'Fanny' Jane née Lutwidge (1803–1851).

Edwin was born on 30 June 1846. His middle name comes from his father's friend and colleague George Heron (1805–1894), honorary canon of Chester, who had baptised his older brother.

Edwin's mother died suddenly at the age of forty-seven, when Edwin was only four and a half years of age. The death certificate indicated 'inflammation of the brain'

The role of looking after the younger members of the family, after their mother died, was entrusted to Fanny's unmarried sister Lucy Lutwidge (1805–1880), who remained with the family for the rest of her life. Edwin's older sisters, particularly Frances Jane (1828–1903), also known as 'Fanny', and Elizabeth Lucy (1830–1916), took some of the responsibility for looking after Edwin as a boy.

There can be no doubt that Edwin's father was very influential in his life, encouraging him to make a career in the Church, and following a 'high church' tradition verging on the ritualistic. Two of Edwin's three brothers were also ordained members of the Church of England.

Charles Lutwidge Dodgson became deacon in 1861, but never proceeded to full priest's orders and never took a parish, instead lecturing in mathematics at Christ Church, Oxford. Skeffington Hume

Dodgson (1836–1919) was ordained deacon in 1865 and priest in 1867, holding a string of curacies before becoming the vicar of Vowchurch, Herefordshire, in 1895. His leaning was towards the broad church with a strong emphasis on caring for the poorer members of his parish, ably assisted by his wife, Isabel Mary née Cooper (1848–1937). Edwin's remaining brother, Wilfred Longley Dodgson (1838–1914), was the more secular member of the family, working for a London estate agent with the Ecclesiastical Commission as one of its clients, before becoming land agent to the estates of Lord Boyne in Shropshire.

In a letter to his aunt, Mary Smedley, a year or so before his death, Archdeacon Dodgson writes about counting his blessings as to the career choices his sons have made or might, in the future, embark upon. In referring to Edwin (who was yet to make his choice) he writes, 'Edwin has so much natural capacity and is so popular and withal so prudent and so very good that I cannot but think he must 'ere long do the same,' thereby indicating his belief that Edwin would also follow a fulfilling career.

Edwin's childhood was relatively insular, surrounded as he was by seven caring sisters who exercised a strong maternal instinct in protecting him from the concerns of everyday life. There are surviving family photographs showing the Dodgson sisters with Edwin among them, taken by brother Charles, who was a renowned early amateur photographer. Edwin's older brother also kept a watchful eye out for him, sending him letters when away from home, and showing a keen interest in his early education. This extract comes from a letter written by Charles to his two youngest siblings, Henrietta Harington (1843–1922) and Edwin, after Charles graduated from Christ Church and then became lecturer in mathematics in 1856 (MS: Berol Collection):

My dear Henrietta,
My dear Edwin,

I am very much obliged by your nice little birthday gift – it was much better than a cane would have been – I have got it on my watch chain, but the Dean has not yet remarked on it.

My one pupil has begun his work with me, and I will give you a description how the lecture is conducted. It is the most important point, you know, that the tutor should be *dignified*, and at a distance from the pupil, and that the pupil should be as much as possible *degraded* – otherwise you know, they are not humble enough. So I sit at the further end of the room; outside the door (which is shut) sits the scout; outside the outer door (also shut) sits the sub-scout; halfway down stairs sits the sub-sub-scout; and down in the yard sits the pupil.

The questions are shouted from one to the other, and the answers come back in the same way – it is rather confusing till you are well used to it. The lecture goes on, something like this.

*Tutor.* 'What is twice three?'
*Scout.* 'What's a rice tree?'
*Sub-Scout.* 'When is ice free?'
*Sub-sub-Scout.* 'What's a nice fee?'
*Pupil* (timidly). 'Half a guinea!'
*Sub-sub-Scout.* 'Can't forge any!'
*Sub-Scout.* 'Ho for Jinny!'
*Scout.* 'Don't be a ninny!'
*Tutor* (looks offended, but tries another question). 'Divide a hundred by twelve!'
*Scout.* 'Provide wonderful bells!'
*Sub-Scout.* 'Go ride under it yourself.'
*Sub-sub-Scout.* 'Deride the dunder-headed elf!'
*Pupil* (surprised). 'Who do you mean?'
*Sub-sub-Scout.* 'Doings between!'
*Sub-Scout.* 'Blue is the screen!'
*Scout.* 'Soup-tureen!'
And so the lecture proceeds.
Such is Life – from
Your most affectionate brother,
Charles L. Dodgson

*Edwin Heron Dodgson as 'the young mathematician'*

*'The New Book': Edwin Dodgson with six of his sisters*

# Education and Training

---

At the age of ten, Edwin began his formal education at a private school for young boys run by the incumbent of North Stainley in Yorkshire, Joseph Jefferson (1818–1882), curate from 1851 until 1881. Just prior to Jefferson's move to North Stainley, he had lived with his parents at Sharow, near Ripon, and had run a school with the help of his sister Eliza. Jefferson then expanded his school-mastering business at North Stainley Parsonage with his sister as teacher and a further schoolmaster, Samuel Hairsine, and his wife both assisting with the teaching.

In a letter dated 6 February 1856, from Archdeacon Charles Dodgson to his son Skeffington, Edwin's father writes, 'Edwin began his schooling career on Monday. Your Aunt Lucy, Fanny and I took him in a Fly to Mr Jefferson's at Stainley where we found several boys assembled.'

There is also a record of Edwin's attendance at this school in the diary of Edwin's eldest brother Charles. His entry for 31 March 1856 records:

Went over to Stainley with Elizabeth Lucy, Caroline Hume and Mary Charlotte to take Edwin back to school ...

By 1861, the school had twelve boy pupils, all under the age of fourteen years, although Edwin had moved on by then.

An entry in brother Charles's diary for 30 December 1857 indicated that Charles was making arrangements for Edwin to change schools. He noted, 'Wrote to Kitchin for my father, to ask if he will be able to take Edwin at Easter.'

In April 1858, Edwin was sent to Twyford School in Hampshire to continue his education, and Charles escorted him there, as his diary noted:

April 17 (Sat): Left with Edwin for Twyford at 11.30 and reached Kitchin's by about 1.30. I could only stay an hour, as I had to be at the Winchester station again by 3.30. Collyns, Jimmy Dodgson, and Edwin, walked there with me. Reached Oxford about 8.

On a previous visit in 1857, Charles had been most impressed by the style of schooling that the headmaster had established:

December 18 (F): I like very much the system of freedom and intimacy which prevails here between masters and boys; though there must often be a risk of the boys passing over the bounds of the respect due to their masters. It is quite the system of ruling by love, and with a master like Kitchin seems to answer well, but I should doubt if there are many in whose hands it would succeed.

Charles knew the headmaster well. George William Kitchin (1827–1912) was a Christ Church man, graduating in 1850 and becoming headmaster of the preparatory school at Twyford, a position he held until 1861.[1] Members of Christ Church were often invited to visit the school, possibly to help with the teaching. Charles made at least three visits to Twyford, one prior to Edwin's transfer there, and two later visits during the summers of 1858 and 1859 when he took the opportunity of photographing some of the pupils, Edwin among them.

The Twyford School records indicate that Edwin made good progress at school. At the end of his first term he was second in a class of eleven boys according to examination results, his friend C Turner coming first. By Christmas 1858 Edwin's achievement was recorded as 'optime'. He did sufficiently well to gain a place at Rugby School two years later in April 1860.

---

[1]  The two other Dodgson boys, Skeffington and Wilfred, had also been pupils at Twyford School, but under a different headmaster.

One letter written by Edwin while at Twyford survives, an undated letter to his sister Margaret, which is full of irony and wit typical of a bright twelve-year-old:

My dear Madgy,

Many thanks for your letter which I am expecting every [day] and am getting rather impatient so I think I will thank you before it comes. Now for news. Last Wednesday we had the reward of the half year (we have one every half) which was that all the boys that were good walkers walked to Bishopstown, a distance of 5 miles (and my venerable self was among the number), the rest went in a fly. Well when we had got to Bishopstown we all went by train third-class to Southampton. When we had got there we met a captain of a yacht and went down with him to his yacht and all of us got on board and after some time the sailors (who by the bye were all called Joe) hoisted the sails and away we went out to sea. Well when we had sailed for about an hour we came to a castle on an island (I forget the name of the castle) where we landed but as the yacht could not go within an hundred yards of the shore we had to go to shore in a boat which we had towed behind us all the way. I forgot to say that as we came out of the docks at Southampton we saw a steamer which had just come from India. All the sailors were being marched about on deck to exercise themselves. We also saw another steamer which the Queen had sent as a present to the King of Egypt but which he had sent back to be repaired. It was being painted afresh and looked so jolly. We also saw the man-of-war ship which had fired the first shot in the Russian war. You have no idea what a size a man-of-war is. It had got 3 lines of cannon on each side of it. Well when we had got [to] the castle we first bathed and then had dinner, and after dinner I and some others went to talk with a coastguard sailor who we found there. He said he had been to the Baltic in the man-of-war I have mentioned before and that he was in some battery or something when it was blown up and he was blown 20 feet into the air (very pleasant) and was blind for 2 months after it but has recovered now. He is now a coast guarder and he has to walk about by the sea a great part of the day with a telescope, and all night has with 3 more men to go out in a boat armed with muskets and things to look out for smugglers. He was a very handsome strong looking man. Then about 4 o'clock we started off for home again and when we got to Bishopstown I walked the first half of the way home and drove the other half. We got home at about 7 o'clock after having spent a very pleasant day. Now I shall expect a very long letter in answer to this, so mind you send me one. But why don't you write to me oftener? It is now beginning to be that I write more letters to you than you to me whereas at Stainley it used to be just the contrary. So mind, I shall expect a letter at least 2 times a week, so mind what I say. Now I will conclude with best love to all. I remain

Your most affectionate brother,

Edwin Heron Dodgson

The letter, quite naturally, says nothing about his progress at school, but concentrates (prophetically) on his interest in naval ships and sailing.

Charles visited Twyford School during the summer of 1858 with his camera and took a number of photographs of the boys, including his younger brother with school friends.

*C Turner and E H Dodgson at Twyford School*

Charles also took Edwin on excursions to London, introducing him to the theatre, art galleries, the Zoological Gardens, and Madame Tussaud's waxworks.

In 1860, Edwin went to Rugby School, following in the footsteps of his brother Charles. It was Charles who escorted Edwin to Rugby for his first days there. This letter (MS: Berol Collection), written by Charles to his sister Mary, sets the scene:

> The Eagle, Rugby
> April 19, 1860
> My dear Mary,
>     Here we are, both safely arrived, and housed at the inn. Edwin's great box has been already sent to the School House, and I have just sent a note to Dr. Temple, asking him what will be the best hour for calling in the morning ...

Charles was clearly acting on behalf of his father, making sure that Edwin settled in, and meeting Frederick Temple (1821–1902), headmaster of Rugby School at this time, to ensure that the necessary arrangements had been made for Edwin's education.

Edwin remained at Rugby for the next five years. A number of letters from Charles to his brother survive, showing his concern for Edwin's welfare while at Rugby.

On the occasion of the wedding of the Prince of Wales in March 1863, Charles arranged for Edwin to have time away from school to attend the celebrations at Oxford. On the evening of the wedding day, Charles and Edwin escorted an important young girl through the city, enjoying the illuminations that were Oxford's contribution to the national celebrations. That girl was Alice Liddell, daughter of the dean of Christ Church, and she was the inspiration for one of the best-known characters in children's literature. Charles was at this time busy writing the story that would become *Alice's Adventures in Wonderland*, published in 1865. Charles recorded the wedding event in his diary for 10 March 1863:

After Hall we went to the Deanery for the children, and set out. We soon lost the others, and Alice and I with Edwin, took the round of all the principal streets in about two hours, bringing her home by half-past nine. The mob was dense, but well conducted. The fireworks abundant, and some of the illuminations very beautiful. It was delightful to see the thorough abandonment with which Alice enjoyed the whole thing.

*Edwin Dodgson as a schoolboy*

# Career Beginnings

Edwin finally left School House in 1864, and appears to have spent some time at the family home before embarking on a career. Matters were brought to a head when his father died in 1868. Members of the Dodgson family were required to vacate Croft Rectory for the new incumbent, and Charles, now as head of the family, took a lease on a house at Guildford. He also set about finding a position for Edwin.

Initially, Charles suggested the civil service, and he wrote to Gathorne Hardy, the Secretary of State at the Home Office and MP for Oxford University. Charles was already well acquainted with him and his family. He noted in his diary:

> I have had some correspondence with Mr. G. Hardy about Edwin, and hope much he may be able to get his name put down for examination for a Clerkship in the Board of Trade, in which hope he is now working at Geography, Mathematics, etc.

Charles's enquiry did not result in a post at the Board of Trade for Edwin. However, Edwin was successful in the civil service examination. Writing home to his sister Margaret, Edwin gives news of his training:

> Grosvenor Hotel, Chester
> 1868
> Dearest Maggie,
>     Just time for one line before post to say that I have passed my exam: and come out either first or second I believe. Will write tomorrow. Many thanks for letter.
>     E.H.D.

In 1869, Edwin was making his own efforts to find a suitable career. He wrote to a distant cousin, Thomas Dodgson (1776–1873), a London merchant, seeking his advice about a position being advertised at a City firm. Two letters survive (MS: Francis R Dodgson) that give details:

The Chestnuts, Guildford
November 24 [1869]

Dear Mr. Dodgson,
    I should be very much obliged to you if you could give me any information as to the firm of Messrs. William Hutchison & Company, Ships and Insurance Brokers, of Clements Lane, Lombard Street. They advertised the other day that they had a vacancy for a pupil, and as I am looking out for some employment, I was thinking of joining them. As I do not in the least know whether this is a line in which I should be likely to succeed I need hardly say that I should be most grateful for any information or advice which you could give me. As I am very fond of mathematics I should of course prefer some line of business, which would especially require it. My sister begs me to thank you for your letter about votes.
    With our united kind regards, believe me
    Yours very sincerely,
    Edwin H. Dodgson

Thomas Dodgson pencilled on the letter 'risky trout' after the name of the firm, and from this we can conclude that his reply to Edwin was negative on the position. Edwin replied a few days later:

The Chestnuts, Guildford
November 27 [1869]

Dear Mr. Dodgson,
    Many thanks for your kind letter. After what you say of Messrs. Hutchison of course I shall give up all idea of entering their office, but if you happen to hear of any employment likely to suit me I shall be very much obliged if you would let me know of it. I should be delighted to pay you a visit at any time, but I should not like to make any engagements at present, as an Aunt of mine at Hastings is most

dangerously ill, and the daily accounts, I am sorry to say, give very little, if any, hopes of recovery, so I am sure you will understand my postponing my visit.[2] As we are within such easy reach of London I hope that some day you will be able to run down and see us if only for a few hours.

With our united kind regards, believe me
Very sincerely yours,
Edwin H. Dodgson

A year passed, and still Charles was unable to secure an occupation for his brother. In January 1870 he wrote to his publisher, Alexander Macmillan, on the chance that a position could be found with Macmillan and Company, London. Alexander Macmillan replied that 'nothing occurs to me at the moment that would suit your brother, but if he were in London sometime and could come and talk to me I might perhaps think of something ... It will be a pleasure to me if I can be of use.' This approach also came to naught.

*Edwin as a young man*

---

2    Edwin's aunt, Margaret Anne Lutwidge, died on 30 November 1869 and was buried at Hastings.

Eventually, Edwin trained as a clerk at the Post Office Savings Bank in London. However, Edwin did not settle in this role, and in 1871 he entered Chichester Theological College to train for the ministry. Charles noted in his diary for 23 September 1871:

> Last Wednesday I heard from Edwin the all-important news that he has decided on taking Holy Orders. May God bless his labours as a clergyman!

At Chichester, Edwin was ordained deacon in 1873, and priest in 1874. There is some evidence that he took a training position at Birmingham before becoming curate at Odd Rode, Cheshire, from 1874 to 1875. From there he became curate of Helmsley, Yorkshire, from 1875 to 1877, and then at All Saints, Shrewsbury, from 1877 until 1879.

Then a major change occurred in his life. He decided to become a missionary to Africa. Part of this was due to circumstances beyond his control, as this letter to his sister Margaret indicated:

> All Saints [Shrewsbury]
> January 27, 1879
> Dearest Maggie,
>     Better late than never – the last week or two has been a most worrying time to me for different reasons, but chiefly because we cannot any longer blind ourselves to the most unpleasant fact that this Mission is at present too poor to support *two* clergy – the accounts of last year show a deficit of nearly £130. Fortunately our stipends were guaranteed for two years, i.e. to the 31st of March, but after that the *whole* expense of the Mission depends on the Offertory, and besides this by the death of the Vicar of Bayston Hill[3] we lose £100 a year, so the long and the short of it is that I must leave All Saints at the end of the Quarter – it will be a bitter trial to me as I am so thoroughly settled and domesticated here, but there is no help for it, so I do not doubt but that there is work waiting for me elsewhere, which will be shown to me in due time. At present I am entirely in the dark as to my future plans. I have for some time past

---

3   In the diocese of Shrewsbury.

had a strong inclination to join Bishop Steere at Zanzibar,[4] but I cannot possibly afford it, so I must be content to wait. The distress here is still very hard – during this month we have been giving out relief tickets of various kinds at the rate of about 18s a day,[5] but now our Funds are almost exhausted, so altogether my life just now is by no means a bed of roses. Please thank Loui [sister] very much for the blankets which are *most* acceptable. I am awfully worried and bothered and my head is in a horrid state, and as it is rapidly approaching midnight I think I must shut up. I hope Aunt L. [Lucy] is going on well. Much love

   Your very affectionate brother,

   Edwin H. Dodgson

Despite his concerns, Edwin was successful in obtaining a position working with Bishop Edward Steere of the Central African Mission in March 1879.

---

4   Rt. Rev. Edward Steere (1828–1882), ordained 1856, missionary at Zanzibar 1862, created third Bishop of the Universities' Mission to Central Africa in 1874.

5   Shillings in pre-decimal money are equivalent to 5 new pence each, with 20 in the pound.

# Zanzibar

---

Edwin made a visit to see his brother Charles at Christ Church, Oxford, and on 11 March 1879 Charles noted in his diary:

> Edwin arrived, to be with me one night, on his way to Guildford. He leaves for Zanzibar next week. In the evening about a dozen or so of the Mission Association assembled in the New Common Room to meet him … Edwin made a little speech, very fluent and sensible.

Behind this entry is a brotherly concern about Edwin's speaking abilities. He suffered a minor speech impediment that affected most members of the Dodgson family. Charles himself had a speech hesitation that was noticeable when reading and speaking, less so when in the company of friends. Six of the sisters had speech problems at varying degrees of severity. All undertook speech therapy at various times in their lives.

In 1879 the Universities Mission to Central Africa (UMCA) appointed Edwin as an assistant at the Kiungani School in Zanzibar, East Africa, a large school for boys who had been recaptured from the slavers. Edwin set sail for Zanzibar, as Charles noted in his diary for 20 March 1879:

> The sailing being put off to Friday [the following day], we spent the day in town, and went on board the *Arcot*, in the Victoria Docks, in which Edwin is to sail: and finally wished him goodbye at Waterloo Station …

The *Arcot* took Edwin to the Mediterranean, through the Suez Canal (which had been open for almost ten years) and across the Red Sea to Aden. While he was aboard the ship, he wrote to his sister Margaret, giving a vivid account of his journey. The letter, although dated April 5, 1879, was written over the course of some days (MS: Amy Irene Jaques Collection):

S.S. Arcot
April 5, 1879
Dearest Maggie,

I got your letter all right when we arrived at Algiers – many thanks for it. We hope to be at Port Said tomorrow night (Sunday) and as today is calm enough for writing I will answer yours, for I don't think we shall stop at the Port very long. Aunt L's present which awaits me at Port Said will be *most* acceptable. I got no letters at Lisbon when we arrived on the Tuesday night after we sailed leaving again on Thursday morning. The Captain says that they will probably be sent on board when he calls there on his way home in about three months! We got to Algiers last Sunday morning at about 7 o'clock and as we were not to set off again till 2 p.m. we got on shore as soon as possible hoping to be in time for the early Celebration at the English Church. My smattering of French came in very handy but when we got to the Church we found that the only Celebration that Sunday was after Mattins,[6] which was to take place at 10.30. I found Mr. Boys the Chaplain[7] at his hotel and gave him Arthur's letter, and we went with him back to the Church and sat in his private room there till Service time. He wanted me to preach a Missionary Sermon, but I declined as I wasn't the least prepared. We had a very nice Service – it is a pretty little Church – some ladies formed the Choir and one of them played a harmonium. I read the 2nd Lesson and two other English Clergy helped in the Service. One was a Mr. Bly (or some such name) who said he was a cousin of the Longleys. There were about 200 in the congregation – chiefly English visitors – and about 40 Communicants.

After Service we (i.e. Geldart, Bellingham and I)[8] were introduced to Colonel Playfair[9] our Consul General and we breakfasted with him and Mr. Boys at the Hotel – regular French breakfast – no tea nor coffee – only Claret and cold water – some queer fancy meat

---

6   *Mattins* is morning prayer in church, an alternative spelling for *matins*.
7   Herbert Arnold Boys, chaplain at Algiers 1875 to 1889.
8   Geldart and Bellingham were probably ordained colleagues, but they are not positively identified.
9   Robert Lambert Playfair (1828–1899), Consul General of Zanzibar 1862–67 and of Algeria 1867–1896.

dishes – prawns – wild asparagus – strawberries – dates and oranges. The prawns and strawberries were delicious, but I didn't care much for anything else and I should have much preferred some coffee and eggs. It was then about half past one so we came back on board, but found that we should not start for some time so after making a hearty *English* luncheon we went back on shore and explored. It is a most picturesque place – no two people are dressed exactly alike. The Arabs are remarkably handsome – both men and boys – I can say nothing about the women as they are kept packed up in white linen except their eyes and the tips of their noses. Geldart and I ventured to go into a Mosque after first taking off our shoes so as not unnecessarily to offend the Mahometans [Muhammadans – Muslims]. The hardship is not great as all the floor is thickly covered with Turkey carpet and matting. There seemed to be some sort of Service going on as a lot of Arabs were squatting round in a circle and continually kept up a wild kind of chant swaying their bodies from side to side in time with the music. The music was very monotonous and their voices very harsh. Scattered about over the floor were a good many men engaged in private devotion, and sitting, standing, kneeling and constantly prostrating themselves and kissing the ground. The building itself was like a large, highly decorated, hall with a shallow stone bath at one end in which some men were washing themselves, and a large raised platform in the middle, with steps going up to it and a railing all round it. It was empty when we were there so I don't know what it is used for. Nobody took any notice of us as we walked about, but I confess I felt a little nervous lest they should resent our presence there. They looked so very wild and fierce.

When we came out we found a splendid French Military band playing in the square, which we listened to for a bit, and then spent the rest of our time in being rowed about the harbour as it was extremely hot. I am keeping my watch at English time for curiosities – according to *your* time it is now about 6.30 p.m., but by *our* time it is 8.30 p.m. – rather a difference! I am trying to write this in the Saloon, but the air is so intensely hot that I must go up on deck again and finish this letter tomorrow on deck by daylight. It is a most lovely moonlight night but awfully hot. I wonder what sort of weather you are having. I'm afraid I shall not be able to *answer* Port

Said letters till we get to Suez. *This* letter will leave Port Said by the French Mail on Wednesday, but I've no idea when it will get to England. Good night for the present.

(Sunday 1.30 p.m.) This morning by the Captain's permission we had an early Celebration in the end of the Saloon, which was curtained off, at 7.30. Afterwards we had Mattins and Service on deck at 10.30 – a pretty good Congregation. We could only muster a few hymn books, so I chose 2 hymns, and we wrote out some copies last night – 'How Sweet the Name' and 'When I Survey'. They went capitally and we had a very hearty Service. It seemed rather queer to have two men at the wheel in the middle of the Congregation. I hope we shall have as nice Services next Sunday (Easter Day) as we shall probably be going through the Red Sea then. Most of the crew are unfortunately Buddhists – the Captain is professedly a Roman Catholic, but he says that when he has no Clergymen on board he reads the Church of England Service himself, and if there happen to be any Roman Priests on board they retire to the other end of the ship in the meantimes – a queer arrangement. We have a lot of queer insects come on board now. We are keeping a good look out for mosquitoes, but as yet none have appeared to torment us. Every now and then strange little birds unlike any English ones come on board for a rest. It is great fun sometimes when we get among a shoal of porpoises to watch them playing about the ship like long black pigs. We are all getting rapidly browned by the sun. I am getting on first rate with Swahili. I know enough now to take a real interest in doing it. It is by no means difficult really though it *seems* very complicated at first. I don't know when next I shall be able to send a letter to England, so you mustn't expect one till you get one. We hope to reach Zanzibar about the 30th of this month. The Consul of Algiers, who used to be at Zanzibar, told me that the country there is most lovely and the climate very enjoyable, *but* he said 'I wouldn't go through the Red Sea in the month of April even if I should be made Governor General of India' – a pleasant look out for us!

Special love to Aunt L.

Best love,

Your very affectionate brother,

E. H. Dodgson

On Saturday 19 April Edwin boarded the *Punjamb* and sailed round Cape Guardafui, along the coast of East Africa, on his way to the island of Zanzibar.

Fortunately, a series of letters written by Edwin to his siblings survive (MS: Amy Irene Jaques Collection) which give us an insight into his life as a missionary in Africa. These letters were copied and circulated among the family, keeping everyone abreast of Edwin's news. The first letter is dated 2 May 1879, recording Edwin's arrival at Ukunazini, Zanzibar:

> We left Aden on Saturday (April 19) in the '*Punjamb*', which is a good deal more roomy and comfortable for passengers than the '*Arcot*'. After rounding Cape Guardafui we saw no more land for a week: so you can imagine how awfully monotonous the voyage was. At last on Monday afternoon we sighted Pemba and then Zanzibar. I really *couldn't* describe the beauty of the scenery as we steamed quickly along the side of the island for about 30 miles before we came to the *town* Zanzibar – the most luxuriant groves of tropical trees and shrubs right down to the water's edge – palms – cocoanuts – mangoes – bananas – and lots of others in all directions and the spaces between filled up with long wavy grass and shrubs. As the coast is a rather dangerous one, with coral reefs etc., we had to anchor for the night out at sea. I couldn't sleep much, though for a wonder the ship was pretty quiet, and at daybreak on Tuesday morning we set off again and reached the town at about 10.30 a.m. The Bishop came off in a boat and came on board. I took a fancy to him at once – he has got a most delightful face and a long black beard. Mr. Johnson,[10] one of the Mission Priests, came with him, he seems very quiet but is said to be a man of great powers. At last we got all our small personal luggage in the boat and made for the shore. On arriving at the beach we had each of us to be carried on shore by natives, as there is no sort of landing stage. We were at once surrounded by a swarm of them of all sizes (I cannot say as to sexes

---

10    William Percival Johnson (b. 1854) of the Universities Mission to Central Africa, who was ordained in 1878, later archdeacon of Nyasa 1896. He built his new cathedral on a swamp and apparently this caused considerable illness among the missionaries.

for I had not then learnt the golden rule for distinguishing men and women, which is, to remember that the *women* are *exactly like* the men, and the men bear a striking resemblance to the women, if you bear that in mind you cannot go far wrong). It seemed to me that anybody laid their hands upon anything they liked and carried it off in triumph and so we walked up through the town to Ukunazini, preceded by about 15 or 20 natives carrying packages. I asked the Bishop if they would be likely to steal more than half our goods – and he said he couldn't say to a package or two, but as a rule they didn't take more than half.

The town consists of houses and huts of every description, apparently having been shaken at random out of a pepperbox, the spaces between are *never* more than about six feet wide, and the only way you can find your way from one place to another is to make out what direction you have to go in and then turn and twist round corners, sometimes only just room to squeeze along – it reminds me more of scrambling about among rocks than anything else, as there is no pretence of levelling or smoothing the ground – the small children literally swarm. The house is close to the Church, which is not quite finished yet, as only half the roof is on, but the Bishop hopes to consecrate it at Christmas. It will be most magnificent like a Cathedral. A small youth about 4, the son of the Kadi (Arab Judge) walked into the room to call. He brought 3 slaves with him – one pretty big boy to carry him when he is tired or there is any wet, and 2 little boys to swell his procession – the little swell himself came and sat on my knee and condescended to inspect my watch and pictures – he only addressed one word to me 'Jambo' (how d'ye do), the slaves squatted on the floor. I patted one of the boys on the head, and he immediately grinned nearly all round his head. After about a quarter of an hour the small youth thought it was time to go so he quickly got down off my knee and signified his wishes to his domestics and they accordingly retired. This is a delightful house – large rooms with verandahs – all the rooms have a quantity of round holes which are appropriated by a quantity of Java sparrows who fly about the house as if the whole place belonged to them – they make nests in the holes. On the first evening a lizard appeared crawling on the wall. I pointed it out to Miss Allen and inquired whether it was a properly authorized inhabitant of the room. She said 'Oh I'm so fond of them, they come from under the pictures and eat the insects. I saw one eating a cockroach the other night.' It suddenly occurred to me that it was time to go to bed so I left, somewhat hastily. Of course, there are millions of mosquitoes who sleep all day and bite all night. By the bye before proceeding further I'll tell you about the human inhabitants of this house, which you will observe is called Ukiunzini; first the Bishop, Rev. C. Maples[11] who is leaving for England tomorrow for a year's rest, next comes Miss Bashford, who came out a month ago, then comes Miss Hinton who has been here some years and takes charge of 18 little slave boys[12] ranging, we imagine, between 4 and 8. They are jolly little fellows and they live in the house, so I see a good deal of them and am good friends with them as far as one can be in dumb show.

We have constant services in the house chapel and the temporary church – chiefly in Swahili, which I am getting to join in pretty fairly already. I walked over to Kiungani yesterday – about 2 miles – a most lovely walk. One of the boys who lived there showed me the way. He could talk a little English and so we managed to converse in a sort of a way. The establishment there consists of about 68 boys and young men – freed slaves – who live together like a school and are taught different trades. A young Deacon is at present in charge, with a lot of laymen under him, each having his own department to look after. The Bishop tells me that he destines *me* to take charge of the place eventually. It will be a very great responsibility, but if the work is put into my hands I've no doubt wisdom will be given me to carry it out. Certainly it would be a work after my own heart, but who is sufficient for these things! We have another establishment about 4 miles off at Ubweni, a village of freed slaves and a school like Kiungani only of girls and young women. By the bye I forgot to mention Miss Allen, daughter of Archdeacon Allen, who lives here and acts as housekeeper and dispenser to the natives. We have queer dishes and things. Beef is the only meat and butter is unknown, but the milk is delicious – also the limeade. We have lots of run honey: I asked the Bishop whether they never had the comb as well; he said

---

[11]  Probably Chauncy Maples, MA University College, Oxford, who went on to become archdeacon of Nyasa, Central Africa, in 1886.
[12]  These boys had been rescued from slavery.

'there certainly *is* comb, but some of it is said to be over a hundred years old.' It seems the bees use it over and over again, and the natives drain it out and leave the comb uninjured for another time.

The sun always sets about 6 o'clock, and it is quite dark in 20 minutes time – no twilight. While we have our tea, the small boys feed outside on the verandah, with a lamp: the effect of the lamp lighting up their swarthy faces, white teeth and dresses, as they cluster round eating curry, is very striking from inside the room, and would make a grand subject for Mr. Whistler's next 'Nocturne'. At this moment there are a lot of natives sleeping on mats on the ground round the house: they have no particular times for food and sleep, but they simply eat when they are hungry and sleep when they are tired. I think during half the time the men sleep while the women work, and during the other half the women work while the men sleep. The young children are awfully precocious: there's a little girl here who used to go and buy things for her mother when she was only a year and a half old!

Please send me as soon as you can four of those musical boxes which turn with a handle – any lively *distinct* tunes will do – they will be *invaluable* for the sick children, for the people here are very musical. I find that any bright pictures are much appreciated, as long as they don't represent *winter* scenes.

In this letter, we see some of Edwin's sense of humour: a family characteristic, which must have pleased his siblings. His ability to 'paint a picture' of his experiences is also imaginative and creative, giving a vivid impression of his life in a foreign country that surely helped his family appreciate and empathise with his new life.

One of the first tasks Edwin undertook was to learn Swahili. Most of the church services were in this language.

He tells us about trips out into the countryside to visit neighbouring schools and homes for the freed slave boys. Edwin was to become the principal of one of these schools. Clearly, Edwin was unaware of the bishop's intention to put him in charge of a school when he arrived in Zanzibar, but, as a further letter dated 29 May 1879 (MS: Amy Irene Jaques Collection) reveals, he rose to the occasion.

You ask for a description of my fellow workers. The Bishop is perfection, he and I are great friends: he has a marvellous gift of being able to superintend the whole work of the Mission, and at the same time to feel real interest and sympathy in the smallest detail of every one's work. He is exactly *the right man in the right place*. He also seems to me to know everything and to be able to do everything with his own hands better than anyone else. The lady workers are – Miss Allen, whose chief work is to keep house in town and to visit the Arab gentry and wives, Miss Hinton, who also lives at the town house and has charge of 19 small slave boys who are too young to come here. She is first rate in her department. Miss Bashford, also in town, she only came out a month before we did, and is very deaf, but she takes charge of a small school of native Hindi boys which is on the increase. She teaches through an interpreter and manages pretty well I believe, but her deafness is very much against her learning the language. There are two ladies living at Ubweni, where we have our girls' school, Miss Bartley who keeps house, and Miss Thackeray who has charge of the school. The workers of the other sex on the Island besides the Bishop are Mr. Randolph, priest, who is Chaplain at Ubweni,[13] and four others who live with me and will be described hereafter. After I had been staying with the Bishop as a guest learning Swahili for about ten days, to my great astonishment he informed me that he intended me to have charge of this place. It is the most responsible post in the whole Mission, and involves the entire charge of about 70 youths, varying in age from 9 or 10 to 19 or 20, I should think, but of course their ages are mostly guess-work. Most of them are freed slaves, but a few are the sons of native princes and chiefs on the mainland, who have sent us their sons to educate. We make no invidious distinctions: in fact I have, for my 2 private valets, a prince, 'Ramatkani', at present only a catechumen, and a freed slave, 'Hugh Patikoli', a Christian. Ramatkani is a splendid boy, of princely manners: he is a capital valet, and very fond of me. Occasionally I squirt him all over with eau-de-cologne, which pleases him immensely. He doesn't know a word of English, except

---

[13]  Edward Seymour Leveson Randolph was chaplain to Bishop Steere 1875–79, and organising secretary of the University Mission to Central Africa in 1897.

'good morning': all our intercourse has to be in Swahili, in which my progress is said to be very satisfactory. I am going steadily on through the exercise book to learn the grammar and rules, besides picking up the language colloquially through personal intercourse. The character which the Bishop gives our lads is as follows:– 'There is no vice with which they are not perfectly familiar, and deceit, untruthfulness, and thieving, are ingrained in their nature.'

I came into office about 10 days ago. About 3 days ago one of our clergy (Phillips) came here from the mainland invalided, and supposing he would have to go home and recruit. He used to have charge of the school here, so we soon arranged a most delightful plan that Williams should go up country to Umba and that Phillips should take his place here under me. I like him very much, and also my other subordinates, Goldsmith who is reading for Holy Orders, and is in charge of the printing office, he is a very nice fellow. The other two are two of my fellow passengers in the *Arcot*, Bellingham, who is over the carpenter's shop and is a steady quiet working fellow, and Geldart who looks after the laundry, and tailoring department, and is assistant schoolmaster.

My title here is 'Bwana Ukubwa' ('great master'), for which office the boys have the most wholesome respect. Our daily routine is
6.30 Choral (Swahili) matins
   7.15 Breakfast
   8 to 12 School and trades
   9 to 9½ Bathing
   12 to 12¼ Recreation
   12.15 Dinner
   2 to 5 School and trades
   3 to 3½ Bathing
   5 to 6½ Recreation
   6.30 Tea
   7.30 Short (Swahili) service for younger boys
   8.00 Choral evensong – after which follows bed.
All talking stopped at 9, except in room of big boys. I am going to make a few alterations – to have Choral (Swahili) evensong, all together, at 7.15 and, at 8.15, 5 minutes silence in the dormitories for private prayer. Certainly a few of the elder boys do understand a little English, but I am perfectly certain very few, if any, can really

take part in an English service, and I mean, if the Bishop does not object, to have all our services in Swahili. I have the most autocratic power to make any alterations I like, but must be most careful not to use that power hastily. I am also planning a reformation in the sick room arrangements. At present the unfortunate sick boys are locked out of the house all night, which I object to.

This is a huge house, with 2 courtyards adjoining with workshops and offices. We have a very nice Chapel, and dining-hall, where we all have our meals together. The boys live chiefly on rice, curry, dried fish, and fruit. They have most wonderful digestions – for, when they choose to be sulky, they very often eat nothing for 3 days, and seem none the worse for it: but they are generally most good-humoured merry boys: they are just like English school-boys in their appreciation of noise and fun. They very rarely quarrel. Most of them carry knives in their girdles, and a few of them have spears or swords of their own, and a musical instrument called a 'zeze', like a guitar, with 3 strings and a hollow pumpkin at the end for a vibrator. The native tunes are very wild, like Gregorian tones. All the natives seem very musical.

I find that all the stock of materials for outdoor games is exhausted, so I am getting up a fresh supply of cricket and football things. On Holy Thursday I gave a general whole holiday. They will have another on Whit Monday as usual, and will probably make an expedition over to Ubweni, to see their sweethearts. Letters are constantly passing to and fro between the two establishments. I had a lot of the lads in my room while I was unpacking, and you would have been amused at their intense curiosity as thing after thing was drawn forth. They are never tired of looking at my photographs and pictures, and take a special delight in the stereoscope, which they call 'a telescope with pictures at the end'. I got my galvanic battery out the other day, and had great fun with it, by connecting it with a pail of water, and getting the boys to fish for small coins therein. The worst of it is that anything the natives don't understand they believe to be witchcraft. All the Arabs in Zanzibar firmly believe to this day that the ceremony of laying the foundation stone of the church was a special charm to make the walls straight. By the bye, remember that any bright button, beads etc. will be immensely appreciated here.

Instead of having to rough it here, my life is if anything too luxurious: I needn't do a thing for myself that can possibly be done by a boy. Ramatkani brings me a cup of coffee at 6.00 a.m. He then makes everything ready for my toilet, even to pouring out the water for me to wash in. We have most sumptuous meals – any quantity of fruit at any time – oranges and bananas all the year round, from 20 to 30 for a penny, and through most of the year pineapples, 3 for a penny: mangoes, dates, guavas, grapes, and many more fruits, to be had for a mere nothing. Any quantity of capital fish. It is certainly rather monotonous to have no meat except beef. We have lots of ducks and fowls at 4*d*. or 6*d*. each. No potatoes, butter, or cheese, but the milk is excellent though it doesn't keep sweet long enough to cream. You soon get used to having everything covered with black ants, who also congregate in the tea, coffee, lemonade, or soup. There are lots of snakes about – most of them said to be harmless: the only two I have come across have been venomous ones – one, which we killed yesterday, very much so. Scorpions also abound: also centipedes: and rats about 4 times the size of English ones. There are supposed to be a few leopards and panthers on the island, but they have not paid us a visit. There are any quantity of wild dogs, who slink about through the woods during the day, and go about howling through the night.

I feel so perfectly settled here, that English life seems a sort of dream – it is so utterly unlike life here. I should never have ventured to volunteer for the position of Head of this place – the responsibility is so great – but as the Bishop has chosen to put me here, of his own accord, I have the great comfort of feeling sure 'as my day, so will my strength be', and it would be a want of faith for me to shrink from it.

Couldn't you send me some linen scrap-books of coloured pictures?

In this letter we discover that Edwin arrived well equipped for his new position. The whole Dodgson family and various friends contributed a range of useful items that Edwin could bring with him, and it was these that caused much interest among his new charges. A list survives identifying most of the donors of the items; a key to the names is given at the end.

| | |
|---|---|
| Priests Bag | 5 Sisters |
| Pocket Surplice in case | CC & MCC |
| Capock | FJ |
| Cap & Gown | LL |
| Writing Case | Guild boys |
| Travellers companion | boy (J Matthews) |
| Revolver | WLD |
| Binocular Telescope | LL |
| Tool Chest | Wilcoxes |
| Knapsack (with fittings) | LL |
| Case cup, folding knife and fork | LL |
| Pocket filter | LL |
| Compass | Mrs. Ford [landlady] |
| Thermometer (self registering) | Mr. Ford |
| Medicine chest | CLD |
| Homeopathic medicine | CLD |
| Hurricane lamp | LL |
| Dressing case | ELD |
| Housewife | LF |
| Etna Kettle (with spirit burner) | HH |
| Jack knife | LF |
| Travelling ink bottle | MAA & LF |
| Carte album | MAA & LF |
| Gobang board etc. | HH |
| Foreign station[e]ry | LF |
| Needfuls for accidents etc. | |
| Deck chair | LL |
| Air cushion (spoilt) | LF |
| Scent spray | CH |
| Flask of eau de cologne | |
| Invalid drinking cup | LF |
| Pr. framed scrolls | |
| Cross with text | |
| Folding bookcase | LF |
| Bible with concordance | boy (Randall) |
| New Test. in separate vols. small | LF |

| | |
|---|---|
| Neale on Psalms. 4 vols. | FJ |
| Williams devotional Comm<sup>ty</sup>. 8 vols. | LF & MAA |
| Pioneers and founders | LF |
| Rowley's University Mission | CLD |
| Daily steps tow<sup>ds</sup> Heaven | Mr. Slatter |
| Hints on parochial missions | Mr. Drayton |
| The Earnest Churchman | A. & M. Wilcox |
| Working for Jesus | Aunt Eliz. |
| Christian Year with photos | Mr. Trimmer |
| Homeopathic Vademecum etc. | CLD |
| 4 books light reading | FJ |

following him:

| | |
|---|---|
| Life of Bp. Selwyn | LL |
| The Waverly Novels | CLD |

*Key:*

| | |
|---|---|
| *LL* | *Lucy Lutwidge* |
| *FJ* | *Frances Jane* |
| *EL* | *Elizabeth Lucy* |
| *CH* | *Caroline Hume* |
| *LF* | *Louisa Fletcher* |
| *MAA* | *Margaret Anne Ashley* |
| *HH* | *Henrietta Harington* |
| *CLD* | *Charles Lutwidge Dodgson* |
| *WLD* | *Wilfred Longley Dodgson* |
| *CC & MCC* | *Charles and Mary Charlotte Collingwood* |

One of Edwin's first tasks was to appoint a deputy, and he chose Mr T Phillips, a clergyman who had previously worked at the school but moved to the mainland. He was invalided back to Zanzibar, but seemed capable of helping Edwin run the school, and he had the character that Edwin was looking for.

*Rev. T Phillips with some of the boys at Kiungani School*

Life initially was very comfortable for Edwin, and there was no shortage of boys to act as his helpers and servants. The following letter (MS: Amy Irene Jaques Collection), written to his sister Louisa over the period of a month, and reproduced here in full, gives a clear picture of life for Edwin at the Kiungani mission.

Kiungani [Zanzibar]
July 2, 1879
Dearest Loui,
    Many thanks for your letter, which I wasn't able to answer by last Mail as I was so pestered with continual attacks of fever, so I fear I only sent a very shabby literary contribution to England. I must do better this mail. Ever since the mail went last Saturday I have been entirely free from fever and have been taking the opportunity of laying in a stock of strength with great success, but as I am not

allowed yet to exert myself at all either physically or mentally I think I might as well *begin* my answer to your letter, which will have to take the form of a running diary for a month. I will just refer first to your letter and see if there is anything that wants answering. You want to [know] about the floral arrangements. I haven't been here long enough yet to know the *exact plan* of proceeding which the trees have adopted of keeping up a supply of green leaves – but it certainly *is* always summer – for the coldest day is only about 10 degrees lower than the hottest – and the trees *are* always green. Some kinds bear fruit all the year round and others have their special seasons, i.e. mangoes, pineapples, guavas, cloves, and a few more, which is rather pleasant and makes them all the more enjoyable. I've got very fond of bananas now and eat lots of them, but sugar cane I still maintain is *disgusting*, as also are *all* the native vegetables, except rice. I have just invested in a tin of strawberry jam and one of plum to take quinine in! They are expensive luxuries, as of course they are imported from England, but quinine is so *insufferably nasty* that it requires strong measures to make me take it at all. The Hodgsons have arrived but I am considerably disappointed to hear that there is *no* package for me. I thought you were sending some things out to me, but better luck next time. Haven't you got any letters to forward to me from Shrewsbury? I have not received any letter from Mr. Smith.[14] Geldart had a long letter from him this Mail in which he utterly ignored my existence! It is very strange!

I am so glad to hear such a good account of Aunt L. – if she could only *get* out *here*, I expect she would very soon be wonderfully well? You can form no idea of the *marvellous* beauty of this island. On moonlight nights – 'when the children are asleep' – the view from the roof really almost realises my idea of the Garden of Eden. There is something so wonderfully *clear* and almost supernatural about the moonlight in the tropics. I have never seen anything the least like it in England.

I have nearly got over the first feeling of *overwhelming* responsibility at having the charge of all these boys. For the first two nights I was here I don't think I slept *at all* from simple anxiety! I do

---

[14]  Samuel Albert Smith (b. 1848), curate of All Saints, Shrewsbury 1877–82.

indeed feel how utterly ignorant and helpless I am as to the right way of dealing with my 'children' particularly now while I can neither talk to them (except to a few who know a little English) or understand them, but I also feel that in answer to my prayers I am divinely strengthened and guided all through the day. The two texts which are chiefly in my mind are 'Without Christ you can do nothing' and 'I can do all things through Christ, which strengtheneth me'. I should *so* like to have them illuminated and mounted sometime either separately or on the same card to hang up. I have a class of the six Teachers (native boys) every Monday for a catechetical explanation of the Gospel for the week in English. I find that by speaking slowly and using simple words and expressions, they can understand me very well, and they really are *very* attentive and answer very fairly, but of course their intellectual powers are very much below the average English schoolboy 5 or 6 years younger than *they* appear to be, and this we always have to bear in mind in teaching them.

(July 3) (No more fever and strength rapidly increasing). When I first came here I thought all the boys had exactly the same face, and were only distinguishable by their height, and I find all visitors think the same – but by degrees I began to see differences between them in expression and feature, and now I find that I can learn to know each single boy just as easily as English boys – but I was puzzled for a very long time between 'Cornwallis' and 'Penyewe'. I *couldn't* see the smallest difference between [them]. This went on for a long time and I was almost in despair, till one day I accidentally discovered that the *two* boys were really *one*! 'Cornwallis Penyewe' – sometimes he was called one name, and sometimes the other. All the boys who have been baptized have got, of course, a Christian name as well as their native one. I always try to call them by their Christian names, or (when there is more than one of the same name) I use both names, but amongst themselves the lads almost invariably use the heathen name only. The English name bothers them for so many of our sounds they *can't* produce. When they see 2 or 3 of us Europeans together they are very shy of coming near us, but if they see me sitting down, they are pretty sure one by one to come sidling up to my side and climb about me … I think you would get very fond of them, as I have done … They seem easily impressed, but they are very shallow and the impression soon fades away. They are much more easily taught by outward *acts* of Ritual than by *words*, and I *think* the teaching takes a firmer hold – at all events the more *Ritual* there is in a service, the more attentive and *outwardly* reverent the boys are – of course I can't see their hearts. It *is* such a comfort to be free to use just as much Ritual as you like without the *least chance* of all that quarrelling and snarling which there is in England.

Unfortunately we have no Chasubles etc. – except at Migila [Mwera?] on the Mainland. At present only the Bishop's Copes, so I must be content to wait, but I am very anxious to wear full Eucharistic Vestments here to add all possible dignity to the Celebrations and not to have to *Celebrate* in the same plain Surplice and Stole that we wear for every other Service. I'm sure a *special dress* will teach our Natives more than anything the unique dignity and solemnity of that Service. The Bishop has two magnificent Copes which he Celebrates in as a rule and also wears at any great functions, when he also has his pastoral staff carried. *Our* Bishop is a *small* man, but the Bishop of Madagascar, whom we have just had here is a most splendid looking man and looks a Bishop, every inch of him. I wonder if you will see him while he is in England. I liked him very much the little I saw of him.

I was very much surprised to hear of Menella Dodgson's engagement.[15] I suppose it is all right, but *I* can't understand how any man can really love *two* wives at the same time.

If matters go on all right here, I don't think there is much chance of my going to the Mainland for the present, so I shall be able to write to you I hope regularly once a month. The other night as we were sitting on the roof in the moonlight we saw crowds of men walking along the shore all in the same direction and one of the boys told us that they were the Banyans (heathen Indians) going to have a burning and so it turned out to be for presently we saw four men coming along carrying the corpse on a board, and others carrying bundles of firewood. We couldn't see the actual burning, but next day we found on the shore the pile of wood still smouldering and the heap of bones and ashes left for the tide to wash away. The plan

---

[15]  Menella Frances, daughter of Uncle Hassard, married Thomas William Bischoff in 1879; she was his second wife.

is this – they first arrange some large flat stones on heaps of sand – on these they pile up a layer of firewood – on this they lay the corpse – then more wood. When the flames have died down they lay upon the ashes a pudding of some kind and a broken water jar. We found the water jar, but the pudding had gone. I fancy it is eaten at once by the wild dogs or the sea birds. They try to have their burnings by night as the Mahometans hate them and persecute them as much as they dare. I mean some night if I have a good opportunity to hide myself somewhere near where I can see all that goes on. I saw the remains of another burning the other day for they have them along the shore 3 or 4 times a week. The Banyans are the only people here who practise cremation.

I am putting down in my pocket book from time to time things that I find the want of and can't get here. I will send it you when the Mail goes.

(July 9) (No more fever and perfect health returned). We have just had an exciting scene. A young slave boy has just come here in irons – he has run away from his master and tells us that his master has stolen a boy, who ran away from here a few weeks ago for fear of being thrashed for stealing, and is keeping him in irons. We immediately wrenched off the poor little fellow's irons and sent him off *under safe escort* to the Bishop who at once forwarded him to the Consul and in a very short time we had the pleasure of having our own boy returned to us and his would-be master locked up by the Sultan's orders awaiting a public flogging, which is the greatest indignity that can possibly be inflicted upon an Arab. The other boy is in the Consul's hands. He told me on Sunday that he had not yet had time to make out whether he was a lawful slave or not. Fancy an *English* Consul being obliged to recognise certain slaves as being *lawful*, and having to give them back to their masters! I met a gang of slave children the other day carrying loads of earth, with a drover behind them with a long whip in his hand, urging them on and shouting at them just like a lot of cattle, and yesterday I met a poor little fellow going out somewhere for his master with those brutal leg irons on – I suppose he had made an attempt to run away – it does seem so *hard* that we have to see all the horrors of slavery, and not be able to do anything to stop it – *how* it can be right for us Christian Englishmen to allow slavery to continue here, when we could put an entire stop to it by using that political power which God has entrusted to us, *I* cannot understand. However, if I once begin to write about slavery I shall go on all day, so I had better stop at once.

Last Sunday I preached my first Swahili Sermon at the early Celebration and then an English Sermon at Mattins and in the evening I gave myself a treat by going into town to the English Evensong and preaching for the Bishop. You don't know what a treat an *English* Service is to me. I can take a Swahili Service and understand it pretty well, but as I *never* have an English Service here on principle, it is a great treat to get away now and then and enjoy the old familiar Mattins or Evensong. My present work is to examine two European 'Readers' for Deacon's Orders and if they pass to present them for Ordination in September. One of them is living in the House here and is the head of the printing department. I gave him two papers yesterday, which he answered *excellently*. He is going to write a Sermon for me this week and then *he* will be all right. The other is on the Mainland, and I have never seen him. He comes down to stay here in a few days to affirm the Ordination. I didn't know that I should have to act as the Bishop's examining Chaplain when I came out here!

You talk about our *Hospital*. The fact is that for the present we have not got one – one of the two professional nurses died, and the other has to be sent back to England for misconduct, and I really do not see much need of one. Of course, we have sick rooms here for the boys, also at Mbwein [Mwera?] for the girls, but we very rarely have a case of serious illness. Just now the returned runaway boy is in a very feeble state from, I imagine, having been half starved and ill treated while he was in slavery – but we have been feeding him up [with] porridge, soups, and pudding and all sorts of good things, so I think he will be all right again soon. I thought he was dying at first. He was like a living skeleton, and did nothing but sleep. He *ought* properly to have a flogging for running away and stealing my note paper, but the poor child has been punished so severely already that I am more than satisfied. I don't think he'll run away again in a hurry. After our lads have been with us some years, very often their natural restless nature makes them want to go out in the world on their own account and get work and they ask me for their certificate of freedom so that no one should dare to enslave them. They generally write in Swahili but I got one the other day written in English. I suppose in consideration of my ignorance. I enclose it for you. Some weeks ago I called him a good boy for some act of obedience, and he seems still to remember it. You needn't return it. If I remember I will enclose also some clove leaves which both smell and taste delicious. I would also send you some banana leaves only as they are about 8 feet long and 1 foot broad they would not easily go in a letter! Will you let me have the recipe for that lemon syrup stuff you make. I wish you could see the butterflies here – they are most gorgeous – also the birds in some parts of the Island. The most objectionable animals here are scorpions, centipedes, snakes, and those insufferable torments, mosquitoes. The wild dogs never show themselves by day, but howl horribly at night. They are great cowards, but it is said they will attack a man if they are a good number together and they are particularly hungry. I have seen one skulking about sometimes. They are nasty looking beasts. We caught a chameleon the other day and watched it change its personal appearance in various ways. It sat on the end of a stick and after the exhibition was over it climbed a tree with much gravity and deliberation.

(July 10) Still in perfect health. We are having glorious weather now. I think the heat is slowly but surely increasing every day, and it will go on doing so till about Christmas.

(July 15) Still in perfect health. We had a funeral here last Saturday. The Bishop found a poor woman – a runaway slave – lying outside our Town Home on Thursday morning apparently dying. They took her in and did what they could for her, but she died on Saturday morning and the Bishop sent her body over here to be buried in the unconsecrated part of our graveyard. The Natives never use coffins here, but the body is sewn up in matting and tied upon a plank and so buried. Of course I couldn't use the Office but we sang a hymn over the grave 'That Day of Wrath, That Dreadful Day'. Last Sunday I gave my second Swahili address on the Lord's Prayer. I have written a letter to Mr. Smith in which I have elaborately explained every possible circumstance on which he might have got some wrong notions, and as I have written in the most conciliatory way I hope it will put matters straight again.

I have been and am still making some rather sweeping reforms here in regard to the management of the commissariat department, which has thitherto been left entirely in the hands of a native Steward, who I am more and more convinced has been robbing the Mission most shamefully, and also – which I confess *I* care most for – has been cheating the boys out of a lot of their food. *Now* I have ousted him, and made a first lieutenant a Deacon-Schoolmaster store keeper. He is working with a will, and instead of seeing scanty platefuls and discontented faces, I now see plates well filled and faces beaming with satisfaction – much more pleasant sight. I have also caused to be abolished certain huge unsightly pails which used to stand on the tables for the boys to drink out of like a lot of pigs, and substituted tin mugs, which they fill from the aforesaid pails of water now banished to recesses in the walls. As they eat with both hands, they manage to get all their food eaten in about 10 minutes and then many of them recline (un) gracefully on the tables and *sleep* till we Europeans have finished, and I am ready to say grace. I wonder if I shall *ever* be able to teach them civilised manners! Luckily it is of no great importance to change their native habits in such matters. They had *spoons* once, but they never could be taught to use them. On Fridays they are regaled on shark, which they are very fond of, but the smell of which sickens me every week.

The English Mail is due here next Tuesday or Wednesday. I hope I shall get a good budget of letters *and* boxes. I shall keep this letter open till after it has come in as the Mail *for* England will not leave till the Saturday after, so that I shall be able to answer anything that wants answering. The Boys have just finished tea and are gone out in the dark for a little play before Evensong in the yard. Their present amusement is to sing in full chorus the tune of 'So Early in the Morning' to some words of their own invention accompanied by some battering on large tin cases and making altogether the most fearful row. It is a very common occupation for the native men to sit for hours together on an empty box and to thump it in a sort of rhythmical way with their hands in silence. Sometimes when there is plenty of moon they spend the *whole night* in this way! Our lads are immensely fond of football, which they play most energetically, though *how* they manage to kick the ball without breaking their toes is a mystery to me. If you could only hear the *row* they are making at this moment you would be assured that past slavery has not crushed *all* the life out of them. I have just commissioned a man to get me a gazelle to keep as a pet and then our household pets will consist of 3 monkeys, 1 Comba (a sort of mixture of a large ferret and a squirrel), one gazelle and one enormous tortoise (which the boys ride on occasionally), a splendid cat and numerous pigeons. These lastly have been wont to live in the store room amongst all the food. I thought this plan was open to objections, so we have had a proper cote made for them and wire netting put over the store room windows to keep them out. I think you will have no course to complain of the brevity of *this* letter at all events – and really by keeping a letter always on hand it lengthens out without any trouble. Why don't you Guildfordites do the same thing for *my* benefit? Though I feel thoroughly settled here and sure that I have found the work which is intended for me to do, yet you have no idea what a treat the arrival of the English Mail is. When it is getting due we most of us have an attack of what we call 'mail fever', much restlessness and application of the eyes to telescopes sweeping the horizon. Even the lads share in the general excitement, for they enjoy immensely to watch any box unpacked – their curiosity is *unbounded*.

(July 21) Another break – on looking closely into the commissariat department we discovered for certain that our Native Steward had been robbing the Mission most systematically and outrageously, so he was dismissed at a day's notice and everything now goes on in a wonderfully smooth way. We have much greater abundance of meat and drink at a considerably less cost – over a pound a week. The Bishop tells me that I have already succeeded in doing what he had been trying to get done for 5 years! I am very glad that I have really been able to do *something* for the good of the Mission, for my small knowledge of the language makes me feel rather helpless. Last Saturday afternoon I felt a little unwell and so went to lie down for a little time. Suddenly I began to shake and shiver as if my bones were coming out of joint. I knew what *that* meant, so I put on my Inverness cloak and waited patiently till the *2nd* stage of fever should come on – the dry heat stage – which it did in about 1½ hours. This was equally unpleasant, though not so fatiguing, and so again I had to wait patiently till the *third* stage began – the perspiration stage. This began in about an hour and was a great relief, so I kept well wrapped up in Inverness and blanket until 10 p.m. – taking nothing but a cup of tea – and then put on my ordinary night clothing in the hopes that I might have a good sleep. But no such luck – I woke up between 1 and 2 with a return of hot fever which kept bothering me on and off all the rest of the night. I was utterly unfit for any work yesterday, but luckily I hadn't intended to preach either at Mattins or Evensong, so those Services and the afternoon Litany and Catechizing were in no way affected by my absence, but I am sorry to say that there was no Celebration, as there was no other Priest here, only a Deacon and 2 Readers – Europeans – who are both, I hope, to be ordained Deacons on St. Bartholomew's Day. Besides taking quinine, I have every day at 3.30 p.m. a cup of coffee with two eggs beaten up in it, which I find refreshes me very much. I hope I shall have quite recovered my usual strength again by the time your Mail goes, but I came down to breakfast this morning and have been doing everything as usual today only feeling a little weak in the head and a little shaky on my legs as a matter of course. *This* attack of fever makes the *5th* in six weeks, so you see I am having a good breaking in.

I have written a long letter to Mrs. Ford by this Mail, which I think will please her. I am refraining from writing to any of my Shrewsbury boys yet as I am waiting to see whether you are going to send me any letters from any of them. Please tell Uncle Hassard some time with my love that Mr. Charles Smith came to see me here some time ago. He seems a very pleasant fellow, and I must go and return his calls on board the 'London' as soon as I am well enough *and* can spare the time, a continuation of circumstances which may or may *not* happen shortly. *Do* you know of any *working Priest* who would come out and join us? We *do* so want some to work on the Mainland and form a new Station. Mr. Rankin has left our Mission altogether, and the King of the Belgian's agent repaid the Bishop his passage money and took on to the Mainland with some elephants for an expedition to find out something or other. I wish Mr. Carter joy of him!

(July 25) (9 p.m.) I have kept this letter open till the last moment so as to be able to answer any questions from you – the Mail was *due* here on Thursday – she generally comes a day or two before her times – but there are no signs of her yet and the Mail for England is made up tomorrow morning at 8 a.m. so our letters *must* go in to town first thing tomorrow. It is very annoying but I hope nothing serious has happened as we have no Telegraph here. We are kept in complete ignorance of the cause of the delay. All the Officials are getting anxious. Dr. Kirk *would* have detained the English Mail 24 hours, only unfortunately she bears sealed despatches for England from Zululand, which are said to be very important, so he *daren't* detain her. I hope there is no letters coming to me which want an immediate answer, for it can't receive one for 7 weeks at least. By the bye if a photograph of this house has been forwarded to you for inspection, please return it to Mr. Geldart, High Street, Crewe, for it belongs to him. *I* can't get one so far, as they are *very* scarce. You might have it copied if you think it worthwhile. Best love to all

Your very affectionate brother,

Edwin H. Dodgson

I hope C. C. is better.[16]

Very sorry – I have mislaid the boy's letter, but will send it next Mail.

The responsibility of his position weighed heavily on his mind, and at times he was anxious about dealing appropriately and effectively with the children under his care, especially as communication with them was not easy. Some of the boys understood a little English, and as time went by Edwin's proficiency in Swahili grew. Edwin's ritualistic upbringing began to surface in his ministry to the boys. He was confident that this approach was more effective both in teaching and in religious education and worship.

In addition to teaching and leading church services (within months he was preaching in Swahili), Edwin quickly found that the bishop had further duties for him to perform, as the letter above indicated. He was asked to help prepare two young men, both Europeans, for deacon's orders, becoming the bishop's examining chaplain (a role which his father had fulfilled for the bishop of Ripon). He was also required to

---

[16] Probably Charles Collingwood, sister Mary's husband.

write testimonials for the older boys, providing them with a 'certificate of freedom' to ensure that they were not liable for slavery in the future.

The management of the school also became Edwin's responsibility, but he found the culture of petty pilfering a difficult one to tackle. In his letter dated 30 August 1879 (MS: Amy Irene Jaques Collection), he wrote:

I have been housekeeper just a month now, and am delighted to find on balancing the books that the expenses this month are about $30 less than last month. I have gone on the principle of trusting *no* one more than I can possibly help, and, as far as I can, acquainting myself with the history of all food *after* it has passed out of my hands into those of the cooks, for honesty seems to be a quality utterly unknown in these parts; so I keep everything – even the milk – strictly under lock and key. I have a regular office for transacting business, which I always keep locked, or I should very soon lose all my pens, paper, etc. and everything else worth taking. As soon as I can talk freely in Swahili, I mean to make a desperate effort to set public opinion *against* stealing: at present it is thought a matter of course! Besides the house work, I have out-door work to see after as well, for I employ ten labourers regularly every day at the rate of 10 pice (about 3½*d.*) a man a day. I am just beginning to build a new blacksmith's forge, as our present one is much too small. It is strange how useful my year's training in accounts has been to me, wherever I have been since my ordination. I couldn't possibly keep things straight here *without* that knowledge, but it is a regular nuisance having to count out such a number of coins – 58 pice for instance! But there is no help for it. There *are* silver coins representing ½ and ¼ rupees, but if I offer one of them to a native, he hands it back with the simple remark 'Haifai' (pronounced 'high fie') which means 'it is no good'.

Our weekly expenses here are about $30 or £16, *not* including meat and bread.

Could you send some large stockings, the commoner and coarser the better – of cotton, *not* wool. My lads are always cutting their feet, and bandages are so apt to come off unless they have something over them: also rolls of surgical or home made bandages would be very acceptable.

By September 1879, Edwin had suffered several bouts of fever, and then a bad attack of diarrhoea, which left him very weak for some weeks afterwards. The bishop came over to visit Edwin, and ordered him immediately to town to be nursed properly. He described his situation in a letter dated 16 September 1879 (MS: Amy Irene Jaques Collection):

> Ukunazini
> September 16, 1879
>     You will be surprised at three things on receiving this – first at the heading, secondly at the handwriting on the envelope, and thirdly at the pencil writing, but all these admit of a very simple solution. Last Thursday morning I was seized with a violent attack of diarrhoea – I thought that probably this would soon pass off, as it had often done before, but as it got worse instead, and I felt altogether getting very weak and ill, on Saturday I sent for a doctor. He didn't come till Sunday afternoon, and evidently didn't understand what was the matter with me as he gave me most confused contradictory directions. The Bishop came over to Kuingani the same day and said I must come in to town and get nursed, so in the evening I had a Bombay chair slung on two poles and got 8 of my biggest boys to come as a double set of bearers – another boy walking in front with a lantern, and Geldart walking by my side. We were quite a formidable procession, and the lads brought me in here and carried me upstairs capitally. The doctor promised to come and see me on Monday, but as he did not appear all day, on Tuesday morning the Bishop sent for another doctor – a German – who pronounced my complaint to be inflammation of the stomach and larger intestines. He sent me mercurial ointment and a powerful preparation of strychnine to be taken every two hours which has produced the good result that he pronounced me better this morning and I have been feeling better all day. Miss Allen is a capital nurse and forbids me to write any more. I couldn't be better looked after anywhere than I am here, so I hope all now will go on well.

But the conditions at Zanzibar, and within the school itself, were far from healthy, and very quickly Edwin's health continued to deteriorate. It became obvious that another, more healthy, position was necessary.

Edwin returned to England, having served only a few months for the UMCA. On 10 December 1879, Charles wrote:

Found a telegram from Fanny with the welcome news of Edwin's arrival. (He left England on the 21st of March, less than 9 months ago).

Edwin spent the next few months recovering his health at the family home in Guildford.

*Edwin in missionary costume*

# Tristan da Cunha

*The island of Tristan da Cunha*

Lying halfway between South Africa and South America, the island of Tristan da Cunha[17] is the peak of a dormant volcano. It consists mainly of cloud-capped, barren, windswept rocks, some 7,000 feet high, rising abruptly out of the sea. The island is about seven miles across and the ground everywhere is hilly or precipitous except to the north-west, where there is a rather narrow strip of irregular plain, about two and half miles long and about a hundred feet above sea level. This area contains the largest settlement, now named Edinburgh.

---

[17] Sometimes written as Tristan d'Acunha – if used in a letter, the spelling is unchanged.

Two smaller uninhabited islands about twenty miles away are named Inaccessible and Nightingale. The former is about four miles square with steep cliffs 2,000 feet high. The latter is smaller, about one mile across, and with two peaks about 1,000 feet high.

Tristan da Cunha was first inhabited by a little band of pirates in 1811, but quarrels reduced their number to a solitary man, Thomaso Corri, who was found on the island when the British garrison took it over in 1816. Stories of treasure which the pirates are reported to have hidden on the island are among the most exciting of its early history. They evidently have some foundation as it is said that Thomaso would occasionally disappear into the bush and return with handfuls of gold, but he died without revealing where the treasure was buried, and its hiding place has never been discovered.

Following the Battle of Waterloo in 1815, Napoleon had been placed in exile on St Helena, 1,320 miles from Tristan da Cunha. The British, fearing that the French might use Tristan da Cunha as a base from which to organise Napoleon's escape, placed a company of soldiers there. When Napoleon died, the company was withdrawn. However, a Scotsman, Corporal William Glass, obtained leave to remain there with his wife and two companions, and they were soon joined by three more. Glass was a well-educated and religious man and turned out to be a wise and capable ruler of the island. Descendants of these early settlers, Glass, Hagan, Repetto, Lavarello, Rogers, Green and Swain, still bear their names.

Before long, Tristan da Cunha was populated by a small community of mixed-race people consisting of sailors who had either been shipwrecked there or had chosen to stay long after their ships had left, and a growing population that had been born on the island. The islanders traded with passing whaling ships and navy vessels on their way to and from the Cape or Australia. William Glass died in November 1853 and he was succeeded as island leader by Peter Green.

In February 1880, Captain East of HMS *Comus* visited the island and reported to the Admiralty that the adult inhabitants were most anxious to have a resident schoolmaster and clergyman, and that they would provide a house and food for his support, but could not pay a salary. The

Admiralty approached the Colonial Office, who in turn approached the Society for the Propagation of the Gospel (SPG), to determine whether they could meet the wishes of the islanders. In addition, a note stated that in 1876 the bishop of St Helena had shown willingness to pay £100 per annum out of his funds to support a clergyman at Tristan, and this offer still stood, but no suitable person had yet been found.[18]

Captain East's report was of sufficient public interest to be published in the *Times*. The Colonial Office received one application to take up the proposed position on Tristan, but it came from Mr Joseph Creese, a married man and a layman. The SPG indicated that the £100 offered was strictly for an ordained man, and could not be diverted to support a layman. Fortunately, within four months another candidate was found. The secretary of the SPG, Henry William Tucker (1830–1902), wrote to the Colonial Office on 21 September 1880:

> Sir,
>
> Referring to your letter of March 27th, 1880, in which you were good enough to send for my information sundry papers relative to the visit of H.M.S. *Comus* to Tristan d'Acunha, I have now the pleasure of informing you that the Society has secured the services of an excellent clergyman, the Rev. E. H. Dodgson, who has been engaged in missionary work in East Africa under Bishop Steere, and who, being unable on grounds of health to return to his former unhealthy station, is willing to become the pastor of the Tristan community.
>
> The Society is responsible for Mr. Dodgson's maintenance and I have now to ask whether the Colonial Office can afford any facilities for Mr. Dodgson being landed at Tristan either by a ship of war from St. Helena or the Cape or directly from this country.
>
> Mr. Dodgson will be prepared to leave England at the end of October ...

---

[18]   Thomas Earle Welby (1810–1899) was the bishop of St Helena at the time.

Edwin said that he responded to a suggestion made by one of his uncles, who had read about the plight of the islanders in the press. Edwin contacted the SPG, and they immediately appointed him as priest in charge (chaplain) on the island of Tristan da Cunha. However, although he was willing to travel to the island at the end of October, the Admiralty had difficulty in providing transport. HMS *Miranda*, a ship of war, had recently visited Tristan, and another would not do so for several months. Edwin was not prepared to wait. He made his own arrangements, using a mail ship heading for St Helena instead.

Charles's diary for 8 January 1881 sets the scene, but he expressed a doubt about the value of such a position, clearly of the opinion that Edwin was wasting his talents:

> Edwin left, about 10½, for Dartmouth, to go on board the *Dublin Castle* for St. Helena – whence he is to go, when opportunity offers, to the small island of Tristan d'Acunha, with a population of about 100. I cannot think he will find this an object worthy to devote much of his life to – with so many thousands in equal need in England.

Writing from the saloon of the SS *Dublin Castle* on 17 January 1881, Edwin gave an account of his journey (MS: Amy Irene Jaques Collection):

> Many thanks for your letter received at Dartmouth. I had no idea I should be able to answer it so soon, but it is so wonderfully calm today, that writing is quite easy here in the saloon. We started at about 12.30 p.m., and then of course the disgusting pitching and rolling began, in less than 10 minutes I had to retire to my cabin from whence I did not appear again in public for four days – it blew a regular hurricane one night and two of our topsails were blown clean away – one of my cabin companions, Jim Muirhead, was as bad as I was, the other, Mr. Lucy, was all right – a very pleasant fellow, married and a gentleman, though *not* a Missionary or a Clergyman – he is going to Natal for a time for his health. Jim Muirhead is a little Scotch Presbyterian about 15 years old, who is

going with his mother and sister to live at Lovedale near Alice in Natal, where the aforesaid mother and sister are going to superintend the Raffir Girls' Industrial School. Jim hopes to get into the Bank at Fort Beaufort – they are all three very nice – and I like them very much especially Jim, who is a remarkable religious boy and at the same time full of fun and cheek, so we get on first rate together.

Of course there was no service on board the first Sunday. On Tuesday morning we touched at Madeira and I crawled on deck while we lay at anchor in the Bay – it is a most lovely Island and an immense number of small boats came off to us full of all kinds of fresh fruits, straw chairs, inlaid boxes, walking sticks and lacework, etc. etc., so in a very short time the quarterdeck got to look like a fancy fair. It was very hot but there was a cool breeze and the scene in and around the ship was very amusing, the Portuguese all jabbering away at the top of their shrill voices. We stayed about 3 hours there – landed a few passengers and took a few fresh ones on board, and then off again.

No sooner were we in the open sea than a regular storm came on and we rolled fearfully, but I had got partly seasoned by that time so I didn't mind it so much and ever since then I have been steadily getting better – the weather getting calmer, and the heat greater, till now today both, I think, reached a climax. I am wearing full Zanzibar dress. Last Saturday night we had a regular musical entertainment followed by dancing – we have about 50 first-class passengers – there are two rather celebrities on board – Mr. Plimsolt,[19] ex MP with his wife and daughter, and Colonel Stewart who was next in command to Sir Garnet Woolsey in Zululand. There is not much need for introduction on board – when a lady sits suddenly down on your knee and you roll over together on the deck it is wonderful how soon the ice of conventionality is broken through. One couple I take especial interest in – the Solomons – she is the daughter of the Bishop of St. Helena and he is a sort of king of the Island – a merchant Prince – he tells me that a small cattle ship is expected from Tristan at the end of this month, so perhaps I may be

---

[19]   This may well be Mr Plimsoll, who introduced the Plimsoll line to shipping.

able to proceed to my destination at once, which will be jolly.[20]
Yesterday I had Mattins and sermon in the saloon at 10.30 a.m., we
chanted the Canticles and sang 4 A & M [*Ancient and Modern*]
hymns.

If the calm weather goes on we shall arrive at St. Helena next
Sunday night, but of course it may be 4 or 5 weeks before this letter
sets off to England. We passed between 2 of the Canary Islands on
Thursday, bleak looking rocks, and sighted the lighthouse of Cape
Verde last night – this is all the land we have seen since leaving
Madeira, and St. Helena will be the next to come into sight, as we
shall not touch at Ascension. We shall cross the line some time on
Wednesday and I believe we shall have some fun by reviving the old
custom of Neptune coming on board and initiating those who have
never crossed it before, happily I have crossed it twice. Now I must
stop this letter and begin another at St. Helena.

On 28 January, Edwin was writing home from Red Hill, St Helena, where
he had been warmly greeted by the bishop (MS: Amy Irene Jaques
Collection):

You will see by the address that I have reached my half-way house and I assure
you I am uncommonly glad to be once more on *terra firma*. As I hoped, we
had lovely weather ever since that gale we encountered after leaving Madeira,
but owing to contrary currents and other nuisances, we were 1½ days behind
time in arriving here, so that before reaching St. Helena on Monday
morning, we had the pleasure of meeting the mail for England, which we
hoped to have been able to send our letters to England by. The consequence is
that H. [Henrietta] will get her letter the same time that you get this – they
will both leave here together on Monday and you *ought* to receive them about
the 18th of February. We are to anchor about 200 yards from the shore at
about 6.45 a.m. on Monday – a lot of the passengers got up about 4 o'clock,

---

[20] Saul Solomon (1817–1892) was an important merchant, born on St Helena but
resident in Cape Town, and MP for the Cape of Good Hope 1854–83. He married
Georgiana Thomson (1845–1933) in 1874, and they had six children, but only three
survived to adulthood. One of Bishop Welby's daughters, Katherine, married a
grandson of Saul Solomon, also called Saul (1840–1896), in 1873.

so as to be able to have as long a time on shore, before setting off again to the Cape, but I took it easy and didn't rise till after we had anchored. On going on deck I found the Bishop and the Colonial Secretary. The Bishop gave me a very warm greeting, and after a little talk we all went down to breakfast while baggage and cargo were being hauled up. The Bishop informed me that I should probably have to wait till *October* before I should have a chance of getting on – as the cattle ship which *ought* to have come here the end of this month had never turned up. All the whalers had gone off, and the Man of War, which is to leave England for Australia in the spring, would never think of calling here unless it had special orders. However he is writing a strong letter by the mail to S.P.G. to urge them to bully the Admiralty about it, so I *may* get off in June.

I like his Lordship very much, he is wonderfully kind and with a great deal of humour in him, and he is a thoroughly good Churchman – he has just built himself a new house, where I am now staying with him, Mrs. Welby and two daughters, all very pleasant.[21] But next Friday fortnight he expects another daughter out from England with her boys, and then I shall have to turn out. He offered me his Official Palace, Oak Bank, to live in if I liked, about 2 miles off, where I should be in solitary grandeur – he never lives there himself now as it gives him sciatica, but keeps a man and his wife there to keep it in order. It appears there are 4 Churches here, his special church, St. John's. He has asked me to take charge of that Church, school and district, chiefly of the lower classes, during my stay, but as Oak Bank is over 4 miles from it and fearfully uphill all the way, I told him that I should much prefer to lodge in the town near my Church, which accordingly I am going to do – to board with Lady Ross, the late governor's widow. I start work there next Sunday. I only have a children's service there, as the Bishop wants me to preach in the Cathedral in the morning and at St. James' church in the evening, but the Sunday after I shall begin my work solely at St. John's. The island is the top of an extinct volcano – the remainder, to a great depth, goes sheer down into the sea. It is all composed of immensely steep hills divided by deep ravines. The

---

[21]  Mary Ann Welby née Browne (d. 1897) married Thomas Earle Welby in 1837, and they had eleven children: Henry Earle (1838–1869), William Glynne Earle (d.s.p.), Charles Earle (1850–1913), Arthur Thomas Earle (1855–1909), Frederick Earle (1858–1900), Penelope, Wilhelmina (d. 1912), Elizabeth (d. 1934), Caroline, Katherine (d. 1937), and Edith Frances (d. 1929).

roads are like spiral staircases on a large scale, and wind round and round the mountains. The scenery is most wild and lovely, quite a different style to Zanzibar. Almost every description of tree and flower seems to grow here wild, from hardy Scotch fir to the tropical Mangoe and Date Palm. The huge boulders, which have been hurled out of the crater, are chiefly covered by prickly pears and scarlet geranium – aloes of different sorts grow in abundance – the wood is used as soap in washing – but no description can the least do justice to the magnificent scenery. In front of the house there is a lovely blue fence of plumbagoes (Mrs. Welby says she always calls it the lumbago hedge). Yesterday morning, after we had arranged for most of my luggage to be stowed away ready for re-shipment, the Bishop handed me over to one of the Clergy, Dr. Lambert, to take care of me for the day, with instructions to bring me up here in time for dinner in the cool of the evening. He is headmaster of a sort of Government Grammar School, besides having parochial work as Vicar of St. James.[22] Yesterday the heat in town in the shade was 85 degrees but at Dr. Lambert's it was only about 75 degrees, and here, not much over 65 degrees which is delightful. The population of the Island, about 6000, is I should think the most mixed in the world. There are pure specimens of English, Scotch, American, Chinese, Japanese, Hottentots, Malays, Africans of all sorts, Indians etc. and every variety of combination of these races. It makes me feel quite nostalgic to see swarms of black boys, just like my Zanzibar ones, but alas clad in English shaped garments, and speaking nothing but English. They are all descendants of freed slaves. The people from Tristan occasionally pay St. Helena a visit and are very highly spoken of on all sides. Two or three young fellows were here very lately. They are said to keep very much to themselves and to be very quiet and well behaved while here. We have both the night and day mosquitoes here – the day ones chiefly busy themselves in the town, and the night ones up here, but neither party have any objection to working overtime to any extent, which is very accommodating of them. Now I must stop.

Best love, etc.,

E. H. D.

---

[22] Joseph (or John) Christopher Lambert (b. 1841), headmaster of the school at St Helena before 1879, SPG missionary 1879–86, ordained deacon 1879, priest 1880, vicar of St James 1880–86, canon and precentor of the cathedral, St Helena, 1881–86.

Edwin's hope that an American whaler would take him to the island of Tristan da Cunha was unfulfilled. To his regret he found that none were available. However, an English schooner, *Edward Vittery*, by chance had called at St Helena looking for a cargo of oil. Finding none, it offered to take Edwin to Tristan for £35, a voyage of ten to twelve days. Some accounts indicate that the SPG chartered the schooner for £40, on Edwin's behalf. In either case, Edwin noted that the captain agreed to take him 'on prepayment of a very large sum of money – considerably more than the expense of a passage to England.' In his own personal account of his time on the island, entitled *Eight Years at Tristan d'Acunha*, he wrote:

> The crew of this schooner consisted of a mate, who would have been much smaller if he had ever been washed – a boatswain, who also acted as cook, his sole qualification being that he knew nothing whatever about cooking – and two apprentice boys. There was only one cabin in the ship, which contained no bed, but the crockery was kept there, and a very strong smelling cheese.

Edwin arrived at Tristan da Cunha on 28 February 1881. His adventures were relayed to the Dodgson family in a letter dated 2 March 1881 (MS: Amy Irene Jaques Collection), which he wrote to his sister Fanny; these letters were circulated, and sometimes copied, so that everyone knew how Edwin was progressing. It was probably some months later before they received this fascinating account of life on Tristan da Cunha as Edwin Dodgson found it.

> Dearest Fanny,
>     At last I have really landed here! I can hardly realize it yet, it seems so strange but I had better take things in their regular order and tell you about the voyage etc. The Captain of a small Schooner of 100 tons agreed to bring me over from St. Helena. We set sail on Tuesday afternoon February 15. Captain Yore had his wife with him and his Schooner the *Edward Vittery* is famous for her speed and he hoped to have got me here in about a week but alas our hopes were doomed

to be disappointed and we were 13 days on the passage, only arriving here last Monday February 28. From the time of leaving St. Helena till the following Sunday I was as usual completely *hors de combat* and lying in misery on a bench in the one little cabin. The Captain and his wife slept in a little house on deck. I had no bed so had to make a sort of one on a bench – with a pillow and a couple of blankets – but oh wasn't it hard, and didn't my bones ache! My cabin companion was a huge, very strong cheese, a most charming companion in sea sickness and the Schooner had just been carrying a cargo of railway sleepers coated with creosote to preserve them. The result was that the delightful creosote flavouring had penetrated through everything including the cases of biscuits. I should have been simply starved if the Captain hadn't taken some potatoes on board and a few tins of lobsters at St. Helena. The cook had but one fault and that was that he hadn't the *faintest* idea of cooking – the salt meat was detestable and the water was dirty, but we had a little preserved cocoa and milk. On the first Sunday some dolphins came round the ship and the boatswain managed to harpoon one – and *didn't* I enjoy a little fresh fish – but that only lasted for one day. But the next Sunday a school of porpoises came round and we managed to harpoon one splendid fellow about six feet long, and on Monday morning I had a tremendous breakfast of porpoise meat. It was really most delicious. I don't think you could distinguish it from tender beefsteak. On Saturday a heavy rain and fog came on, and as the Captain knew we were close to these Islands *somewhere* and he couldn't tell exactly where he was as there was no sun visible, he got very anxious. On Saturday night he suddenly found himself in smooth water, which showed he was close to land – he couldn't see it and he told me his 'heart was in his mouth' till he found himself amongst waves again. On Sunday, when the sun came out, he discovered that he had just shaved the coast of Tristan during the night. I saw the Island for the first time on Monday morning – we also saw the other two islands – 'Nightingale' and 'Inaccessible' at the same time. It was very interesting as we got nearer the Island to see the green vegetation beginning to appear, then the grassy plains and then the houses and cattle.

A boat soon came off to us, for, as the Captain had dressed the ship with flags in honour of me, the people couldn't imagine what was the matter till they came alongside, and then for the first time I was introduced to about half a dozen of my new parishioners, such fine, healthy, bright honest looking young fellows – all as clean and bright as a new pin. After talking with them for a few minutes I put my small portmanteau into their boat, and some of them immediately rowed me on shore – leaving one or two of their number to come on shore afterwards with Captain and Mrs. Yore. They brought with them on board a lot of apples and bottles of new milk, which were very acceptable. I was munching apples all the way between the ship and the shore. As I neared the beach I saw a whole crowd of men and boys waiting to receive me, and on landing I met with a most warm welcome, and nearly had my hand shaken off, and then all marched up together in a sort of triumphal procession to the houses, a few hundred yards off over rugged ground and little streams of fresh water. I was straightaway conducted into one of the houses and sumptuously regaled with delicious tea and bread and butter. This was about 2 o'clock in the afternoon. The Bishop of St. Helena had sent with me a Pastoral Letter to all the Islanders addressed to Peter Green, so after sitting in Joseph Bertham's house, an old Yorkshire kinsman, for some little time, they got all the heads of the families together at Peter Green's house, and I went up there too. Peter Green is a very venerable looking old man, about 73 – he is the oldest man on the Island, and the only great grandfather! So, though he does not claim any authority he naturally has a sort of patriarchal influence over them all. He read the Bishop's letter to them all in which I was introduced to them as their 'Vicar' – and then I said a few words of greeting to them which was very well received. And they all eagerly promised to do all they could to make me comfortable and happy, and so far they have certainly kept their word.

For the present I am domesticated in old Mrs. Cotton's house, where I have a very comfortable bedroom, and all my regular meals, but I find that at every house I go into at any hour of the day, I am expected to eat *some* sort of a meal – tea, coffee, milk, bread and butter, fruit etc.

I have now been here 3½ days and already I am getting to feel quite at home among the people and their shyness is rapidly wearing off. The climate is most delicious and the people seem at present at all counts to be living in clover. They make first-rate butter and bread, with milk, and there is any quantity of prime beef, mutton, pork, geese, fowls, fish, apples, peaches, grapes, potatoes, cabbages, tea and coffee. They say they have not been short of flour for many years now, though they grow no corn.

There are 106 people altogether including myself – 17 different families, 54 males, 51 females, loads of children, and loads of huge dogs, which were rather alarming at first but they have got used to me now and are getting quite friendly. I was warned at first that if I would stand my ground when they came at me I should be all safe, but that if ever I began to run from them 'it would be a chase'. I am thankful to say the latter alternative has not eventuated *yet*. Every family has four or five of these huge brutes – half mastiff, half bulldog – so you may imagine that as I walk about I have to run the gauntlet of a good many.

Captain and Mrs. Yore are also staying on shore for a few days while the Captain is buying bullocks and other things to take back to St. Helena – everybody appears to live more in other people's houses than in their own. It is most confusing to a stranger to know who lives where. I find a lot of people in one house and I tried at first to connect them in my mind *with* that house, but on going into another house, lo and behold there is the same lot there! So I have given it up in despair.

On Monday night we had a regular jubilee in the house, about 40 of the people assembled and after the supper the table was cleared away and we had a lot of singing and dancing. They all seem very musical and most of them seem able to play the violin, accordion or concertina, and all three by ear, and they dance beautifully – it is quite a treat to watch them. We kept it up till about half past 12 and I can truly say you would never see better behaviour in any English drawing-room. I see that I shall have no difficulty in getting a player for my harmonium in church. I have just arranged with one of the men – Jacob Green – who has about the best house in the Island, to agree to give his house for the present to be turned into a temporary church. Luckily he has no children and he and his wife have been taken in as guests by another family. We are going to take down the partitions and I think it will really make a very decent church. I shall also have the use of it for a school. In that case I shall somehow screen off the Atlantic with a curtain or something – all the men have promised to set to as soon as possible to build a regular church of stone as soon as they can get blasting powder. I *hope* a man-of-war will call in here about June and then I shall try my best to get the Captain to supply us with powder and we shall go ahead in fine style. I find there are 4 babies to be baptised. I am rather puzzled about some of the marriages which have been performed by the Captains of whaling vessels. If they had performed the marriages *on board their own ships* it would have been all right, but unfortunately most of them have *come on shore* to many of the people where they have *no power whatever*! The people have of course thought it was all right until they asked me, and of course I was obliged to tell them the truth. I feel perfectly certain they are really married in the *sight of God*, and with that I think we must rest content. I tell them that such a marriage would be utterly null and void in *legal matters* – but that won't matter much in the present case – if ever they *wish* me to remarry them I shall do so without scruple.

I found that there were no school books for me at St. Helena, but as I didn't like to come over here without any, I bought some at St. Helena, and it was lucky I did so, as I found that all copy books etc. have come to an end here. I shall have a school of about 40 children I expect to teach regularly, besides a lot of the elders who seem to want to improve their learning. The women knit any quantity of wool stockings. They take the wool right off the sheep's back, wash, card, spin, and knit it splendidly.

Best love, your very affectionate brother,

E. H. Dodgson

Many of Edwin's plans came to an end within a few days of arriving at Tristan da Cunha. Another letter written home, dated 11 March, explained the circumstances (MS: Amy Irene Jaques Collection):

My prospects of life here have suddenly changed altogether! I told you that the schooner kept hovering about the island day after day, waiting for favourable weather to come to anchor and land my baggage, and to take in a cargo of bullocks, etc.

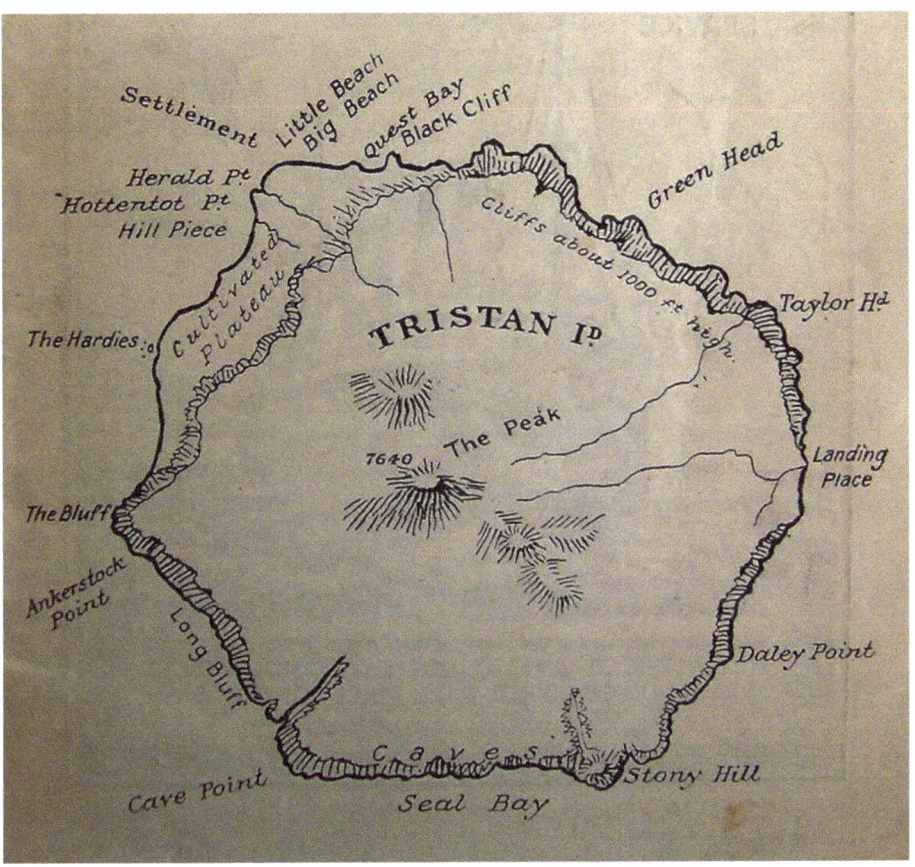

*Map of Tristan da Cunha*

Last Tuesday morning I was standing talking by one of the houses, where it struck me that the schooner was *very* near the shore. The Captain was not on board, and while I was standing looking at the ship, he came running past me in a great state of anxiety – he got 4 of the island men, and they went off in a boat to get on board. I thought it would be all right as soon as he was on board, and that he would find some way of getting her off. I then went in to dinner, during which one of the boys brought in word that the boat was coming back from the ship. This was a great relief as we thought all had been put right, but directly afterwards we heard that *another* boat had left the ship with all the crew! This sounded very alarming. The Captain's wife rushed down to the shore. I followed more leisurely, and just missed a terrible sight – the boat, containing the Captain and four of our men, had got within a few yards of the shore, when a breaker rolled in from behind, and made it turn a complete summersault, turning all the men out. Fortunately those on shore were able to rush into the water and get them out safe – but the second boat was rapidly nearing the land, and you may imagine the breathless anxiety with which we watched *her*. It was thought hardly possible that she should get in without being turned over in the same way but by God's mercy she did come in safely, and landed the 4 sailors and 2 ship-boys who formed the crew.

The Captain then explained that they couldn't get the ship away from the shore, as the current kept drawing her in, so they had let down 3 anchors (all that they had) and hoped that they would suffice to hold her safe till the wind changed, and they could sail her off. She was within a few yards of the rocks, but while the cables held, she was safe. But it was not to be. One after another the cables parted, and she drifted straight on to the rocks, and we knew of course that she must go to pieces. The sea was very rough, and the ship was hurled from side to side in a fearful way. We could hear her timbers cracking. There was nothing to be done except wait and watch till she broke up, in hopes that some of the things on board might be washed on shore.

I can't describe my feelings as I sat on the cliff, watching her breaking up. It seemed like a hideous nightmare. Things have been coming ashore ever since, as she went more and more to pieces. Four or five of my boxes have been picked up, more of less smashed, the two trunks of clothes, my book-chest (the wood was all broken away, but the zinc held the books together, though it was a good deal torn), and one or two other things, including, I am thankful to say, the case of church furniture, linen, etc. Also the box containing the font, and its oak stand, and also the oak lectern.

I am trying to save a few of the most valuable Divinity books (that is to say, the insides of them for, of course, the backs are off) but I'm afraid it will be no use.

I have also taken the photos out of my large album, in the hopes of their drying without coming to pieces – the album itself was simply pulp. The box of books from the R.J.S. was very little damaged. About 6 out of 21 packages have been washed on shore, and with the exception of clothes, linen, etc. about nine-tenths of their contents are ruined – so you see I have to start life here in a very different position as to worldly possessions to what I expected. But it is so clearly God's will that I should begin my work here in a state of comparative destitution (except as regards clothes) that I feel to care very little about it.

It is strange to be writing here on the 14th of March, and to have no idea how long my letters will have to wait for a chance of leaving the island. Then, of course, they may have to go all round the world before they reach England!

Strange to say, the Sunday before the ship went ashore, the Captain had to go on board, and he brought off with him my case of Communion wine, as he feared the sailors might be tempted to break into it, and as I have also got the vessels, etc., God has provided us with all the necessary means for Celebrations, for which I am indeed most thankful. I am very sorry to say that my 'Priest's bag' which you all gave me, was washed on shore smashed, and broken open, and with the contents washed out – but one of the glass cruets came ashore by itself, uninjured. The 11 volumes of Keble's sermons which Charles gave me, have come ashore. They were so tightly packed together, the insides were hardly wet at all, and now that they have been out drying in the sun and air for some days, are all right, except in appearance. It was melancholy work unpacking boxes of *slush*, and the shore was covered with bits of books, etc., from the wreck.[23]

*April 6.* You see this letter has been 'on the stocks' for some time. There is very little left of the *Edward Vittery* now – nearly all the timber has been washed on shore, and hauled up by the people for firewood, etc. The oak slab for the top of the altar has come on shore unbroken. I am having it put on legs, and shall use one of my red blankets for its frontal.

I hope to have our first Celebration on Easter Sunday – a good many of the older people were confirmed in Mr. Taylor's time, by Bishop Gray, so that I have been having special services twice a week, to prepare for Holy Communion both those who have been confirmed, and those who have not. So I hope there will be a good number of Communicants at Easter. I shall begin by having only Sunday Celebrations, but hope to have them oftener when the people have really got to value Holy Communion.

---

[23]  The site of the shipwreck is known to this day as 'Down-Where-The-Minister-Land-His-Things'.

I have just had a large bell (from one of the many ships who have been wrecked here) fastened up at the end of the school to ring both for school and services – services on Sunday, Matins and sermon, children's service, evensong and sermon, and in the week we have a short service and sermon every Tuesday and Friday evening. After Easter I mean, D.V., to have service every weekday evening, and as soon as I can see my way to it, every morning as well.

The people are all most ready to come to church, and behave very reverently. We have plenty of hymn-books. I adopt the Wesleyan plan of reading out each verse before we sing it, so that all can join, as most of the congregation are very poor readers. My harmonium, alas! was broken to 'smithereens', but I have my little pitch pipe, and we manage to have hearty singing.

I have 45 day scholars, and about 20 evening ones. The first day or two they were all so scared that I could hardly get a word out of them, but they soon got over their first alarm; and being naturally very high spirited, soon became noisy. But after 6 weeks of schooling I have succeeded in getting them into capital order.

Easter Eve – yesterday we had the same services as on Sunday. We have had a service and sermon every night this week. The people have been in the habit of always observing Good Friday like Sunday.

Captain Yore and his wife and crew got off the island about 10 days ago, in a sailing ship going to Australia.

The loss of most of his luggage was a great trial for Edwin, and he clearly felt the loss more than he was prepared to say in letters to his sisters. In his account of his time on Tristan, he gave a little more detail:

There was a horse on board, whose body was washed on shore to the great astonishment of the children, who had never seen one before. Among the many things which I lost were all my boots, so that for nearly a year I had to content myself with home made moccasins made of pieces of the hide of bullocks, dried in the sun. These got so hard during the daytime that they had to be soaked in water all night, and in this wet and flabby condition to be put on in the morning; each pair lasted me about three weeks. I was accommodated with a room in one of the houses (with a sofa bedstead therein), 8 feet long, 8 feet high, and 6 feet wide; there was just room for one chair by my bedside, which had to be upon the bed whenever I wanted to be on the floor. I afterwards got one of the men to make me a small wooden bedstead and some book-shelves in another room, of which I was given the use. I believe it was thought rather greedy, my wishing to have *two* rooms.

Edwin was able to salvage a hundred copies of the *Mission Hymn Book*. The small stone font that Edwin brought with him was later washed up on the beach, and has remained on the island ever since. The schooner was heavily insured, so the captain, who was also the owner, gained a great deal of money as a result of the shipwreck.

Tristan da Cunha had been without a priest for twenty-five years. Mrs Cotton, originally from St Helena, taught the younger children, gave religious instruction at her home every Sunday, and read prayers. It was, therefore, fitting that Edwin should reside in her home to begin with. The 'headman' was Peter Green (real name Pieter Groen), a Dutchman

*Tristan da Cunha settlement*

who had been shipwrecked on the island in October 1836. He taught some of the older children.

Edwin's brother Charles was still doubtful about the value and purpose of this new role in an extremely isolated part of the world. On 7 March 1881, probably long before the above letter had found its way back to England, Charles wrote to a friend and former member of Christ Church (they matriculated on the same day), Richard 'Espinasse (1832–1902), who was then vicar of Westhampnett, Sussex. The letter (MS: 'Espinasse) included this paragraph:

> My brother Edwin made up his mind a year or two ago that his 'call' was to Missionary work, and went to Zanzibar: but the ague[24] was too much for him, and he came back in a few months. He then fixed on the small island of Tristan d'Acunha (about 100 people, I believe) and is now at St. Helena, waiting for a chance of being carried to that seldom-visited place. It is a mistake, *I* think: he might be eminently useful in a large London parish, and I hope he may yet find himself in some such sphere.

Edwin's own personal account, written after his return to England, gives detail of the arrangements made by the islanders for their new vicar:

> The houses are built only one storey high – stairs, I am thankful to say, are unknown – divided into two or more rooms by wooden partitions, and thatched with tussock-grass. The walls are of stone, of which there is abundance on the island, about three feet thick (5 feet at the gable ends) and 8 feet high. The walls are obliged to be made very strong and low, because of the gales of wind ... The house placed at my disposal was turned into a Church by the simple expedient of removing the partitions, and so turning into one long room, which just held all the people. Every family had to provide enough benches for its own members, the wood coming from wrecked ships, and the Vestry was formed at the west end by screening off one corner with a sail. A blue dungaree curtain, cutting off the Altar, made the Church into a school on week days. There was soon a very fair choir of men and boys, and a full choral service, except Psalms,

---

[24] A fever with hot and cold stages of shivering and sweating.

*A cottage on Tristan da Cunha*

twice daily. The choir-boys had to learn the Canticles, Hymns, etc. by heart, as they could not read at first.

Some months after his arrival on the island, Edwin wrote a detailed and optimistic letter to the SPG, which contained these extracts:

There are now 107 persons on the Island, including myself, in sixteen families. I landed here on the Monday, and by scraping together all available benches and filling up with chairs, we were able to have very crowded, hearty services on the Sunday. There are a fair number of Bibles and Prayer books here, and I happened to have on shore a parcel containing a hundred copies of the *Mission Hymns*, so we managed very well for books.

The children are of course very backward compared to those in English schools, but they are naturally bright and intelligent, and very anxious to learn. Besides the week-day schools I have Sunday school every Sunday morning for half an hour, and a children's service in the afternoon; so they get plenty of teaching.

All the people here speak English slightly Yankeefied – as they do a good deal of trade with Yankee whalers. There are a few white families, but most of the Tristanites are a sort of mulatto, with clear brown skins and beautiful eyes and teeth, and woolly hair.

I like them very much; they very rarely quarrel or use any bad language. Drunkenness, I am sorry to say, has a hold on a few of the men when they get a chance. They are decidedly a religious people in their simple way, and I have not the least difficulty in getting them to church either on Sunday or week day.

Besides fishing, whenever the weather is calm enough, their chief occupations are looking after their cattle, sheep, pigs, etc., and attending to the apple and peach orchards, which are about three miles from the settlement, and their potato patches, which are only about two miles off. They get plenty of flour from passing ships in exchange for Island produce, as well as coffee, tea, and sugar; and as there is abundance of milk, bread, meat, potatoes, and fruit, I do not think there is much to fear of my being starved yet a while!

The houses are all built of stone, low on account of the gales, but very substantial, and divided up into rooms by wooden partitions. As most of the men are very fair carpenters, and as there is no lack of wood, etc., from wrecked ships, there is plenty of strong house-furniture.

There is always abundance of beautiful water, and the climate is most healthy. The Island is much more beautiful than I had any idea of. There is plenty of vegetation on the plain at the foot of the mountain, but no trees, except apple and peach trees, in the gullies on the mountain sides. Altogether I feel sure that if the advantages and pleasantness of the Island had been better known, many clergy would have been glad to have come out here.

The men have promised to build a real church as soon as they can get some more blasting powder from a man-of-war to get the stone with.

Edwin wrote to his bishop after six months, giving a report of his work on Tristan thus far. Tristan came within the diocese of St Helena, and Thomas Earle Welby was the bishop of St Helena at the time. Edwin's letter (MS: Amy Irene Jaques Collection) is dated 30 October 1881:

My dear Lord Bishop,

As I have now been working here for more than half a year I think I ought to give you a report of our proceedings. First as to the Church services, there are now 24 communicants in all – out of a population of 107 – 16 families. I had the first Celebration on Easter morning with only 12 communicants, so the number has exactly doubled since then. At first I had a Celebration only on alternate Sundays at 8 a.m., but for the last three months I have had it weekly with an average of 21 communicants. Among the few things which were washed ashore after the wreck of the Schooner was most providentially a case of Church Furniture containing lectern, foldstool, Communion plate, cruets, candles and candlesticks, cross and bases with bunches of dried English flowers and linen vestments, surplices, etc., and as I had already a case of 12 Communion Wine landed safe, we have every requisite for reverently appointed Services and Celebrations. I was bringing out an oak altar in pieces – the slab was washed ashore unbroken, so that I have had a very good altar fitted up with a retable, and two red blankets serve as reredos and frontal. I have fastened an illuminated carol cross on the frontal and the whole is raised on a wooden platform – also covered with red blanket.

We have the best house on the Island as Church and School. I have the East end curtained off with a sail during the week and only taken down for the Sundays and then when the benches are properly arranged and all school materials put away it makes a very decent little Church. The Sunday Services are as follows:

8 a.m. Celebration
10 a.m. Children's Service
11 a.m. Matins and Sermon
2.30 p.m. Children's Service
4 p.m. Evensong and Sermon

On Wednesdays I only have one service at 6 p.m. consisting of a shortened form of Evensong (omitting the Psalms, 1st Lesson, and *Magnificat*, for very few can read the Psalms as yet) and an address on the 2nd Lesson except on Wednesdays and Fridays when we sing the Litany, followed by the 2nd Lesson and address, and on Saturdays we have a short special service of preparation for Holy Communion with a short address.

All my copies of *Hymns Ancient and Modern* are lost but fortunately I had 100 copies of the *Mission Hymn Book* on shore, so that we have one or more hymns every Service though my harmonium is at the bottom of the Sea. But I have a small pitch pipe which does very well to start us. We chant all the Canticles to Gregorian tones – the *Te Deum* to one of Helmon's Chant Services and we sing all the Responses. Most of the young people know the Canticles and Responses by heart – the people are naturally very musical, so the singing throughout is above the average, and *most congregational* – in fact I have never taken part in more hearty Services.

*All* the people come to Church on Sundays including young babies, and on week nights about three-quarters of them on an average, so that there always are good congregations. I am thankful to say very reverent behaviour 'meekly kneeling upon their knees'. They are all very attentive and I try to make my sermons as simple as possible as the people are very ignorant and their vocabulary of words is very scanty.[25]

As to School work I have day School every day from 9.30 in the morning to 12.30 and from 2.30 to about 5 in the afternoon, with about 48 scholars of whom 25 are infants, and I have appointed one of the elder girls who is a *fair* scholar as far as reading and writing are concerned as their teacher, with another girl to assist her with a few of the youngest, and they manage very well. I found the children at first utterly undisciplined and with a very few exceptions utterly ignorant, but by the combined use of patience and *care* I have got the school into very tolerable order and though the children have very little idea yet of using their *minds*, they seem very fond of school – and as they are naturally bright, they are getting on very well. I found a few easy reading books here, slates and slate pencils, but no pens or copy books, so I have to teach writing on their slates with short pieces of pencil. One boy of 9 years old had never learnt to write his letters, but he has got on very well – I enclose his signature which he wrote for me the other day with pencil and paper for the first time. The same boy had never done a sum or made a

---

[25]　He means that they lack knowledge rather than not having the capacity to learn.

figure in his life till I came and he has now got through the simple and compound rules into long division, which I think does him great credit. I think perhaps *he* has made the *most* progress in learning, but most of the others are not far behind him. I give them a religious lesson every morning for about an hour and they are really getting to answer simple questions tolerably well now, but I am afraid that the lesson they *enjoy* the most is the singing lesson, which they get on capitally with. They can sing a great many catches remarkably well and also some two part songs for treble and alto including the National Anthem, which was quite new to them. I have taught a lot of the young men to sing bass to a good many of the Hymns, which was an entirely new idea to them all, but as they are naturally musical they have picked it up very quickly. All during Lent I had a special service twice a week for preparation for Holy Communion and on Easter Eve a good many of the people solemnly renewed their Baptismal vows, as you suggested to me. I have done my best to make them clearly understand that I can only admit them to Holy Communion as being 'ready and desirous to be confirmed' if ever the opportunity presents itself.

I find that nearly all the marriages here for the last 25 years have been performed by American Whaling Captains *on shore*, so of course they have no *legal* force whatever, but it seems to me equally clear that under the unique circumstances of this place any two persons between whom there is no lawful impediment, who solemnly pledge themselves to each other before God with the pledges in our marriage service, are in His sight *truly joined together* and so I have told them. I hope I am right in so doing. One of our men who was married in this way has just gone off in a whaler without giving any notice, merely staying behind when the others left the ship and telling them that they might see him again in six months – his name is Benjamin Green, and as he was one of the three who spent some time at St. Helena last year, he may possibly turn up there again. Another of the young men is going to St. Helena on the first opportunity to be married – he is a very nice steady young fellow – I *hope* he may be confirmed before he returns here, for he will probably have to stay there for six or eight months. Two whalers have already arrived here from St. Helena, but neither of them have brought me anything. The mate of one of them told me that he believed the Captain of the *Eliza Adams* was bringing me some things, but he has not turned up yet so I am living in hopes of soon having my spirits refreshed with tidings from the outer world. I do sometimes feel very lonely and depressed here, but that of course I must expect, and as I have such constant work I feel settled and happy, on the whole, and if it was not for occasional bouts of overpowering headaches, which I suppose are the result of sun-stroke and ague, I should be perfectly well.

Although less than a quarter of the islanders took communion, most attended church service on a Sunday. About three quarters of them attended daily evensong, which included an address by Edwin.

Edwin had forty children to teach, whom he divided up into four classes. Initially, the children lacked discipline and were sadly lacking in their education. Edwin insisted that the parents send the children regularly to school in order for him to be efficient in teaching them – not initially understood by some families.

Through patience Edwin restored order among the children and began to deal with their general ignorance. He found that two of the older girls (sisters) were able to act as pupil-teachers, and they each took one of the classes of younger children, Edwin giving them lessons after school hours. Eventually, he persuaded one of the older women to set up an infant school so that by the time they became his scholars they at least knew their letters, could read some words and were able to count.

Discipline was strict at Edwin's school, and much learning took place in silence. Edwin was pleased to report steady improvements among the children, but nevertheless he had to keep up standards in both learning and behaviour. On Saturday afternoons, he instigated a punishment for children who had, during the week, not worked well, which resulted in their names being put on a 'black-list'. These children had to come to school and stand within certain chalk boundaries, called a sheep pen, and learn by heart a passage from their reading books. Once achieved, they could depart. Some completed it in about half an hour, but others took almost two hours to learn their piece. Edwin reported that the punishment seemed to be very effective, especially among the boys, who disliked it intensely. No payment was made for the school, but in return the parents provided Edwin with firewood.

Conditions on the island certainly suited Edwin's health. In the previous thirteen years, forty-seven children had been born and only six persons had died, and there had been no infant mortality. Mary, the wife of Peter Green, was a skilful midwife. The sanitary arrangements on the island were excellent, testified to by the ruddy and healthy appearance of the residents, old and young alike. In addition, the economical position of Tristan was, at that time, perfectly viable. Ships, chiefly whalers, visited the island about once a month, mainly to procure fresh meat and vegetables. The land cultivated for the potato crop was particularly productive. The island had about 500 head of cattle, with cows producing a good supply of milk. No importation of cattle had taken place for at least fifty years.

The following letter from Edwin, dated 28 December 1881, graphically illustrated the difficulties of receiving supplies from passing ships and the infrequency of visitors. It was sent to Edwin's sister

*Cattle on Tristan da Cunha*

Margaret, whose birthday was on Christmas Day (MS: Amy Irene Jaques Collection):

> I must begin this letter by wishing you many happy returns of your birthday, though you will probably be well on the way towards *another* birthday! I drank your health in milk on Xmas Day. Ever since the arrival of the first whaler here about the end of October I have been anxiously on the look-out for the *Eliza Adams* which I was told was bringing me things from St. Helena, but though *five* other whalers called during the next eight weeks, the *Eliza Adams* was conspicuous by her absence. I had arranged to give the school a fortnight's holiday from Monday the 19th, and on the Tuesday two whalers were reported in sight, one of them turned out to be the young Lady I had been on the look out for so long – she couldn't get within 6 or 7 miles of the shore as it was almost a dead calm, but Captain and Mrs. Howland landed in one of their boats early in the afternoon and he informed me that he had a lot of things for me, and as he was in a hurry to get away again to his whaling ground some hundreds of miles to the Eastward, it was arranged that our boats should take off his beef and potatoes and bring back my things, but alas it got so late and dark that they had to put off the plan till the next morning, but when Wednesday morning came a strong north wind had got up and the sea was 'on the boil' to such an extent that it was impossible to get the boats off. We saw the ship during the first part of the day standing in and out, but towards evening she disappeared and during Thursday – which was a facsimile of Wednesday – we saw nothing of her. On Friday the wind 'hauled round' to the South and the sea got like a sheet of blue glass and we were all hourly expecting to see her standing in again, but no sign of her appeared, and we had mostly made up our minds that if she didn't come in on Saturday it would be pretty certain that she had got tired of waiting and had 'skidaddled'. Saturday came and went with a perfectly smooth blank sea and I had quite made up my mind that I should have to wait for another year before I should have any chance of getting my things, so that by Saturday night I had put the matter out of my head and I was quietly preparing for Xmas

Day, but when I got up on Xmas Day I found that she was in sight about 15 miles off. It was again a dead calm so it was impossible for her to come any nearer, but you may imagine how jolly it was to have hope again revived, but at about half past five in the afternoon we were astonished to see a boat coming ashore, and in about an hour's time two of the mates and half a dozen of the men landed and brought 3 or 4 *small* cases ashore with them – the Mate actually wanted our men to take the 'taties off that night – 15 miles! Of course they refused point blank to do anything so unreasonable so we housed all the men for the night and at about 6 o'clock on Monday morning the ship had managed to get within 3 or 4 miles of the Island, so our boats took off the supply of beef and potatoes Captain Howland wanted and brought back the rest of my things and two barrels of flour in exchange for the provisions. Captain Howland refused to take any money for bringing my things, so I sent him off a fat sheep as a Xmas present and the Islanders gave him besides a lot of potatoes, so I hope he will be ready to bring me things again *next* year. I can't describe my sensations when for the first time after leaving England on January 7 I 'clapped eyes' on a lot of letters in familiar handwriting. I got my *letters* on Sunday night, and if my room hadn't been pretty well crammed with 'humans' I believe I should really have cried with joy! Lambert had kindly dated each envelope with the date of its arrival at St. Helena, so I was able to read them in proper order – it was about 1.30 a.m. before I had got through my preliminary perusal of them. I will answer them in detail when I have mastered the contents, but at present I will only say in answer to a question constantly repeated, that since I left England I have never received *any* letters from *anybody* till now, nor have I had any chance of doing so, so I had a grand accumulation of them to revel in, I think about 40 letters altogether! Some of you refer with disgust to an imaginary incident, i.e. a packet of letters having been taken off in one of our boats to a ship in May and brought back to shore again – it certainly *would* have been disgusting if it had really happened, but it is an absolute fiction – no such thing ever happened to any of my letters. My *first* lot of letters went off to the Cape some time in April, and I never sent you off any others till the beginning of September. Hope you have received this second lot all right. This was a big bundle for each of the sisters for they had so accumulated here for many months.

30/12/81 I find that I have three letters from you bearing dates March 9, May 18 and June 22. If you have written me any others I can only say that they have not come to hand. I am not surprised that the 'New London' routes for letters, etc., have proved a failure, for the New London Whalers have long given up coming here. We must make up our minds to the unwelcome fact that the only way to communicate with me is by St. Helena once a year as a 'chance' ship is a small delusion for even if they do come within sight of the Islands we are not able to communicate with one in a hundred but of course there will be no harm in your chancing letters in this way if you will remember to duplicate any information contained in them by the St. Helena route.

Your best plan will be to write me letters to any extent – English paper much preferred – whenever you have anything to say during the year. Let the letters accumulate in a box till the first mail for St. Helena in September and send the lot off with any books, etc., that have to come c/o Mr. Lambert and write the extra letters by way of 'latest intelligence' by the second mail in September and the first mail in October, which may or may not be in time to be sent off to me that year.

Remember that though my letters may be lying at Guildford for months before going to St. Helena, there is not the slightest chance of any news therein being forestalled, for no other ships ever come here from St. Helena except the Whalers, and they only between the last week in September and ditto in October.

If you carry out this plan there will not be the slightest objection to being 'limited to one sheet' (as one of you write in one of your letters) or in using thin paper. As there are not any stationer's shops here I have to use any paper I can get – this note paper is a present from a Yankee Captain.

In January 1882, the Admiralty diverted HMS *Diamond* to Tristan so that it could deliver books and school materials, and a replacement for the lost harmonium. The arrival of this man-of-war was a surprise to Edwin, as this letter to his sister Elizabeth, dated 2 February 1882, revealed (MS: Amy Irene Jaques Collection):

You can imagine my state of excitement when the *Diamond* came in here on the 21st of last month. She appeared first on the morning of the 20th, but the general opinion was that she was a merchant steamer. She cruised about all that day a long way off the Island up and down in a rather meaningless way as if she wanted to call in but was rather frightened, like a moth round a candle. But at about 5 o'clock in the afternoon she seemed suddenly to screw up her courage to stick point and steamed right in for the Island getting to look more and more like a Man-of-War the nearer she got. So at about half past 6 one of our boats went off to her as it was a lovely evening. I would have gone off in it to call on the Captain, but it was just Church time, so I said that I would go off and call on him the first thing the next morning. We all expected that she would have left England last Spring and been cruising about South America ever since as is the case with most of the Men-of-War which call here. But when our men came ashore after Church I could hardly believe my ears when they told me that she was only 5 weeks from England and had brought a lot of things for me some of which they brought on shore with them including a bundle of letters. They said that the Captain intended to anchor the next morning so that I could go off the first thing. I didn't get much sleep that night, as I was up unpacking and reading letters till after 3 a.m. and then I just lay down dressed for about an hour's snoozing before getting ready to go off to call on the Captain, who I had learned from a letter was a cousin of the Guildford Taylors. We didn't actually get off till after 6 a.m. as the men took off two boat loads of potatoes, sheep, geese, etc. When I got on board the Captain had not yet made his appearance, so I made acquaintance with the Chaplain, a very pleasant young fellow, who was taking the cruise for his health, and the other Officers. It was a wonderful treat having some educated people to talk to for once in a way. In about half an hour Captain Dale appeared and was very friendly. I breakfasted with him in solitary grandeur and then after squeezing out of him no end of presents and also making a few purchases out of ship stores which he had no power to *give*, we made up a party to go on shore consisting of the Captain, Chaplain, and a lot of the junior Officers armed with rifles and guns on murderous thoughts intent with regard to our Albatrosses etc. When we landed I trotted the Captain and the Chaplain about the Island a little, while the youngsters dispersed to try and get some shooting with plenty of juvenile attendants as guides. We got on shore between 10 and 11 o'clock and after showing off our lions my guests had a hasty luncheon at about 1 o'clock and then they went on board again and made off as soon as they could. The Captain was evidently very anxious to get off as soon as he could as he was in rather a 'scare' about our rollers and sudden changes of wind. But I was rather disappointed that they only paid us such a short visit, which however was very pleasant while it lasted.[26]

Very many thanks for your letters and share in the presents. The only things marked with your name on the list are two books, *Sun, Moon and Stars* and the *Revised New Testament*, but I find from your letter of November 9 that the Church books are from Louisa and yourself. They are indeed very very acceptable as I only had a *borrowed* Bible and Prayer Book for Church use, rather shabby, but now I have a set which would do credit to *any* Church. They are so *exactly* the right sort – so *durably* handsome and the Bible *exactly* fits my oak lectern which was washed ashore. I haven't read *Sun, Moon and Stars* yet, nor have I had much time to examine the *Revised Edition* yet. So I cannot say much about them. I see from a file of *Church Times* and *Guardians* that opinions about the value of the *Revision* are very contradictory, so the only thing is to form my *own* opinion. I presume that the long list of books and other things not specially appropriate to any donors are partly general presents and partly purchased on my account for I hope you will consider that you have carte blanche to purchase on my account not only what I order but also anything else which you think will be useful to us, so you need never have any scruples in expending money to any extent. By the bye, I have been terribly remiss in former years as to birthday

---

[26]  Captain Dale also wrote an account of this visit – see below.

presents, but it is never too late to mend, so please each of you give yourselves from me a birthday present each birthday since my departure to the value of 10s. to 12s. till further notice. I hope that by the time you get the letter Fanny will have received a considerable remittance from Mr. Lambert on account of my stipend. I am sending Maynard and Harris a pretty large order for carpenter's tools etc., and telling them to send in the account to Fanny for payment. I hope I shall get about £120 Insurance money as I have done my best to satisfy the 'red tape' requirements before 'shelling out'.

I have established a lending library at Peter Green's house under his charge, as he has nothing much to do in his old age except to eat, drink and sleep, and is besides very fond of reading. So this employment will just suit him. The S.P.G. have sent me a most liberal supply of Bibles, *Hymns Ancient and Modern*, Prayer Books, and School Materials – books etc., so that we are quite set up. And Mr. Tucker has also sent me a very nice little harmonium, which I have had to doctor a good deal as it had been terribly knocked about on the voyage and was very badly packed. Evidently by some one utterly ignorant of which parts of the instrument required specially guarding. But by dint of patience, glue, American cloth and waterproof I have happily been able to repair the damages very satisfactorily. But the case has been so much strained that I fear it will let in a great deal more damp than is desirable, but that can't be helped. I am very grateful for it, as it will be of great use, and also pleasing – your substitute of a clock is a most 'happy thought'. I tried to wind it up each evening for the first two days but I found that it had run down so *very* little that I came to the conclusion that it must be an eight day clock, which has proved to be the case. It is such a comfort to have a time keeper that doesn't want shaking up every few hours as is the case with most of the clocks on the Island. By the bye my Churchwarden is very anxious to buy a *striking* clock, but he cannot afford to give more than about twelve dollars (£2.10). I don't suppose it would be possible to get a good one for anything like that sum, but please choose one on my account if you can get one for about £8 or so, and send it out the first chance. I can then let him have it for twelve dollars and say nothing about the surplus trusting to his ignorance of the value of such things, for as he *commissioned* me to get him a clock I shouldn't like to make him an *open* present of one as it might make *him* uncomfortable and others jealous. I think it had better be a *larger* one than mine – a *louder* strike – only the hours – and a *wooden* case and thus I should think you will be able to get a pretty good one for the sum I have mentioned, but don't go beyond £10 – something after the style of your hall clock, but that probably cost a *great* deal more than *I* am prepared to give. But I leave it to you to do the best you can for me in the matter. Didn't you get a budget of budgets from me on the 24th of last November? I hope you did as Legan got a letter from me on that day which I sent off by the same ship as your budget. If you *did* receive them, you could have answered them by the '*Diamond*' as *he* did, for she was delayed by bad weather and so did not leave Sheerness till December 5th. But from the dates of your letters you do not seem to have known of this delay. So much the worse for me, but as Legan got *his* letter all safe it would be very strange if *your* letters – in the same packet – were lost, so I do not feel much anxiety about them, as *none* of your letters are dated as late as November 24 which was the day on which I hope you got them, and the '*Diamond*' was *supposed* to sail some little time before that date. Please execute *all* my commissions except for school materials and personal wants which you *know* you have already supplied. I find that the only school materials I am now deficient in are half a dozen galvanized iron ink wells to go into the holes in the writing desks, and a frame of coloured balls for tracking counting and other rules of numeration. Please add them to my list of orders and above all things *do be sure to get* a dozen pair of hand wool carders. I think I described and delineated them in one of my letters. They are *very* urgently wanted. If they can't now be got in England they can be got from the United States. If they cannot be bought ready fixed on wooden frames the wire part can be got in rolls and we can 'fix' them here. I think I should like *16* pair instead of one dozen and then I can give one to each family. I believe there are now only 2 pair on the Island and they are nearly worn out. One of Mrs. Cotton's daughters has just knitted me two pairs of socks of home grown and home made wool. They are delightfully soft and warm and do not get chilly and clammy when I get my feet wet, which I do most days. I am quite reconciled to wearing moccasins now that I have found out how to keep them soft (stuffing them into a jug of water when I go to bed and they are all right in the morning).

(9 February 1882) I have begun to read *Sun, Moon and Stars* and I am charmed with it – it is exactly the sort of book I wanted to get hold of so as to give me some simple facts in an intelligible form to cram into the people's minds for I found that none of the young people had the slightest idea that the earth was round or that it moved! So they can hardly be considered deeply versed in astronomy. I am just looking through your four letters dated March 2nd, May 24, October 13 and November 9 to see if there is anything that wants answering. You told me in May that the American Clergyman told you that a ship was expected soon '*from* Tristan' and so you express a hope that your letters *to* me were taken by it – this seems to me *absolutely impossible*. Mr. Trimmer's intended marriage is simply the most extraordinary thing I ever heard of. How any man who has really loved his wife *can* bring himself to marry again is beyond *my* comprehension, but I am not much experienced in married life and widower-hood so I hope it may be all right. Many thanks for the second volume of *Bishop Wilberforce's Life*. I certainly *do* possess the first volume, but it was borrowed by a young shark on my arrival here and has not yet been returned. As to medicines – please thank Charles *very* much for his most acceptable bottle of Calendula – its curative effects on cuts and wounds is marvellous. Also many thanks for the Chloric [looks like] Ashe and other things you have sent me. Please send a good supply of Castor oil, Chlorodyne, and aperients pills in a *glass bottle* well stoppered, Russian glue and glycerine and a few pots of Leibeg – also please add to my list of wants a lot of narrow blue and red ribbon for book markers – some *very* narrow and some rather wider – curtain rings of various sizes and an instrument to open tin lined cases – something like a sardine knife on a large scale. Do you know I have always had a very guilty feeling about that letter which I sent to S.P.G. I hoped that if you ever saw it you would not remark on the date! The fact is some of our men went off to try and catch a passing ship one day and as I had Mr. Tucker's letter fastened up and no other ones ready to go I sent it off fully expecting that I should very soon have another chance of sending a letter to the Chestnuts, but that chance never came so you see in this way *he* got the 'latest' intelligence instead of

*you*. The old linen you sent came in very useful the other day for a Whaler came in with a sailor on board who had scalded one side of his leg and they seemed to have no proper remedies and the Mate who came ashore was very grateful for some linen and some of the jar of linseed oil and lime water which I gave him.

(12 February 1882) I have just finished my Sunday's work and have been reading *Bishop Field's Life* which I am immensely interested in as I have never had a chance of reading it before. Please give my very warmest thanks to Ellen and the other servants for this kind thought of giving me a book. I have received two parcels of books and pictures etc. from two total strangers – one a Rev. G. Victor at Malvern and the other from 'Mary Wilson' at Louth, Lincolnshire. They say they have seen and been much interested in the account of my work in the 'Gospel Missionary'. It is very kind of them. I am doing my best to recompense them by writing them good long letters about this place, which is all I can do. I hope to send you a lot of skins the next time the Schooner calls here, which professes to be going to keep up a regular trend with us and the Cape and St. Helena. I hope the Captain will keep his word, as it will be an unspeakable boon to us to have a regular communication with the outer world at however long intervals. We hope to see him back here early in March so you may get this letter about the first week in April. I am much pleased to hear from Louisa of the improvements in externals in Southwick Church ... I have just had a blue curtain put up in Church to be drawn across the East End during the week instead of the heavy sail which used to be hung up on nails, and which was both very troublesome to put up and take down, and also very ugly when up, so this blue curtain running on tight rope is a great improvement in every way. I expect to have 27 or 28 Communicants this Easter in the place of only 12 last Easter when we had the first Celebration that had been had on the Island for twenty years. Old Peter Green remarked to me afterwards that it would [be] just like Christianity beginning with only 12 Apostles – or words to that effect. The average number of Communicants now every Sunday is 22 and the average Offertory exclusive of my own offering is between five and six shillings, which all goes to the C.A.M. [Central African Mission] so you see I am still doing a little to help that Mission though I can do no more *personal* work in it

and I like my people to get into the way of caring for and helping their fellow creatures. I see the C.A.M. has got a separate Office of its own now. I fear that will involve additional *home* expenditure, though it may be a good thing for the Mission as a whole. Now I must wind up this budget to be ready to go off as soon as possible. Best love.

Your very affectionate brother,
Edwin H. Dodgson

Edwin was pleased to get the new school supplies since he was almost out of slate pencils and other requirements for teaching. He reported that following this delivery he was able to supply a Bible, prayer book and hymn book to every islander who was able to read. He was now able to provide choral matins and evensong daily with an average congregation of twenty adults together with a number of children.

The bishop replied to Edwin's comment about the lack of legal marriages on the island by advising him to take the marriage service, after morning prayer, from the prayers that formed the service, and conclude with a blessing, accepting that their exchange of vows already constituted a marriage 'under their peculiar circumstances'.

One of the great disadvantages of the island was the sudden gales that blew up with little warning and were ferocious in their intensity. Edwin wrote a graphic account of such extremes of weather:

The gales of wind are terrible, they come on quite suddenly, and fortunately only last for a short time, two or three hours – generally at night. I have known thirty head of cattle killed in a single night by simply being blown down on level ground. One evening at service I noticed that there was not a single female in Church – old or young – the congregation was entirely made up of men and boys, though it was a fine evening with a gentle breeze blowing from the North. I wondered at this as it was very unusual. Suddenly in the middle of the service the wind went round to the South-East with a noise like a cannon, and began rapidly to blow up a gale. I *just* managed to walk home after the service – about a quarter of a mile – with the help of two of the young men, but the hail-stones on the back of my neck were extremely painful. The people had thought that a gale was coming on by certain signs in the weather, and so the females stayed at home. A short time afterwards I had to crawl to the Church on hands and knees for the Early Celebration one Thursday morning at about 4 o'clock, in the dark and rain. The gale was rapidly going down, but I had to go much earlier than the other people to get things ready in the Church, instead of five minutes it took me over an hour to get to the Church, and I lost my way! Things look so different when your nose is close to the ground. I believe this constant wind is the reason of the extreme healthiness of the islands, for sickness and deaths, even from old age, were very rare.

The following extracts come from a letter (MS: Amy Irene Jaques Collection) dated 14 April 1882, written by Captain Dale, who travelled to Tristan to bring provisions to the islanders. The letter begins with the difficulties of landing on Tristan da Cunha:

We might have got there two days earlier if the weather had been finer, but as we were getting within a hundred miles the weather was so thick that we lost some time before we could make the island . . .

He went on to describe his meeting with Edwin Dodgson:

We anchored at 7 in the morning and at 8 Mr. Dodgson came on board and breakfasted with me. After which we landed and he undertook to be my guide and showed me what there was to be seen in the island. It is nearly round, about eight miles in diameter, with a central mountain which attained the height of 8000 feet. The settlement as it is called consists of about thirty small cottages scattered over a tolerably level strip of land close to the sea and on which good grass grows and where they pasture their cattle. The inhabitants themselves are a simple though uncultivated set of people, but at the same time seem to have a great appreciation of the value of money. Mr. Dodgson certainly deserves every praise for having so unselfishly given himself up so entirely to improve the moral and intellectual condition of those who he proudly calls his

'Parishioners'. His great aim now is to build a church for them. The building they have in use now being an old cottage converted for the purpose. I gave him ninety pounds of gunpowder towards the work, as the whole of the building material has to be blasted from the rock and as they haven't much mortar they build their houses with huge blocks of stone as the force of the wind is so tremendous as to overturn anything less substantially built. His own quarters are very primitive and one does certainly look on a man of that sort with great admiration as he has given up, by going there, all the little comforts and delicacies of this life, which one is so accustomed nowadays to look upon as necessities. But his great trial must be during the long dreary evenings, when he has no one to converse with. There is no one in the island whom he could make a companion or with whom he could interchange ideas on any subject that would be of interest to him. I supplied him with everything I possibly could from the ship and I should not be in the least surprised if I heard eventually from the Admiralty that I had been a great deal too liberal in giving away Government stores! We only remained at anchor till 3 p.m. and then left on our way to the Cape where we arrived ten days afterwards.

Work began on blasting the stone from the mountainside in order to build a new church. But progress was slow. The men who undertook this voluntary activity had other tasks that required their pressing attention. Only eight to ten hours a week could be spared, and even this was suspended if any ship called for supplies. In April 1883, Captain Fullerton of HMS *Sapphire* estimated that work on building the church would take the islanders between twenty and thirty years to complete at their current rate of progress. Eventually, Edwin realised the futility of this activity and told the people that they could use the stones as a wall for the cemetery. The islanders did, however, provide another house for the school, and this left the shared house for the sole purpose of the church.[27]

---

[27] In June 1922, the stones originally intended for the church but used for the cemetery wall eventually became the foundation stones of the church that now exists on the island.

A letter written to Edwin's sister-in-law Isa, wife of Skeffington Dodgson, reveals that he was looking forward to a break from Tristan life. He wrote on 8 June 1883 (MS: Amy Irene Jaques Collection):

Dear Isa,

Many thanks for your 'combination' letter and for the *Church Bells*. I have had no time to look them through *regularly* yet, for what with School and Service work and private divinity reading I have very little spare time. I had an immense pile of newspapers sent me last Christmas – *Guardian*s, *Church Times*, *Standard*s, *Public Opinion*s, etc., so I first arranged them in months, and I have been steadily in this way reading up the news of last year – which is very interesting to me. I have just got through the Egyptian business – it is absurd to call it a *war*. I see in some of my latest papers which came by the *Sapphire* that the secret-murder society in Ireland has at last been brought to justice but I have not read up that yet. I am very thankful to think that there may now be really an end to those sickening outrages in that unhappy country. Church affairs seem getting into rather a better state too. My friend Lambert writes to me that the new Primate is a 'grand appointment' at which the Record and Rock are tearing their respective hair – he is the one living link between the South African Church and the Church of England as I believe there is an appeal to him from our Metropolitan of Cape Town as being the Patriarch of the Anglican Communion, but the appeal is only to him *personally* and not in any way to the Privy Council, I am thankful to say. I wonder if I shall ever work in England again! I am now in great hopes of getting a 'ticket-of-leave' in a short time and then my own wishes would *of course* be to join the C.A.M. again, but if that was not feasible, then I should hope to work under Bishop Wilbe at Bloemfontein as I had almost settled to do when I was called to Tristan, but 'Dieu dispose'. If ever I *do* get away from here I think I am fairly entitled to spend some time at home before again going on my travels. I can hardly realise what it would be to find myself once more among civilised people who can *use their minds* more or less. Mr. Taylor managed to survive *five* years in this place but that was 25 years ago, and so many years of steady intellectual deterioration must have made a great difference here, and I sometimes feel as if even *one* more year here would drive me *mad!*[28] But I have no doubt that 'as my day so shall my strength be'. When I saw the name of Skeff's curacy after leaving Brailes I shuddered to think that I *might* have to learn its most unpronounceable name, but I am now thankful to know that *that* danger is past. Your present home, whether it be Suckley or Alfrick, has a much more reasonable name! I know the neighbourhood of Worcester and Malvern pretty well. If ever you have an opportunity of going to Newland, a little village about a mile from Malvern, I hope you will visit the Church there. It is a perfect little gem with its inner walls completely covered with frescoes and the Rector, Mr. Cosby White, and his wife, are charming old people. Eichhaum the Chaplain of the Clergy House of Rest at West Malvern is another friend of mine – also Lowndes of Little Comberton near Pershore ... His son went out to Zanzibar shortly after I had returned to England. A Mr. Victor (Curate of St. Matthew's, Malvern) was kind enough to send me a small box of books etc. last year though I have not the pleasure of his acquaintance. If ever you come across any of these individuals please remember me to them. I have preached at Worcester both in the Cathedral and at St. George's Church ... when I was deputation for the C.A.M. What a magnificent pulpit it is at the Cathedral! I quite forget the name of the rector at St. George's, but he might remember mine possibly. But the Dean is far too great a swell to retain any recollection of such an insignificant individual as myself! ...

(16 June 1883) You see there has been a long pause in this letter. I have been laid up in bed ever since Tuesday evening with a protracted bout of over-powering headache, but I was able to do a good deal of reading in lucid intervals, so that the *Heir of Redcliff* and the *Pillars of the House* came in very handy, and it was really a great refreshment to be able to spend a few uninterrupted days with *educated* characters in those books ... I lived on tapioca and sago. I feel a good deal better today, but my head is still so weak that I rather dread tomorrow's Services. If I only had a Curate I should be

---

[28]  Edwin's isolation, exhaustion and bouts of ill health were making him frustrated and depressed. This frustration occasionally shows itself in comments like this, where he is uncharacteristically harsh about Tristan and its inhabitants.

strongly tempted to absent myself from everything except the Celebration.

(20 June 1883) My headache still haunts me like a most attentive ghost. I wish I knew how to exorcise it. I have just remembered another connection I have with the diocese of Worcester. I was confirmed by the Bishop at Rugby in the year 1862, but as to the best of my recollection he was *then* an old man. I wonder what he looks like now for I have never seen him since that day. I think that I will fill this envelope with a short letter to Skeff in answer to his and then I shall feel that I have done my duty as far as you two are concerned – at all events for the present. I wonder if you have set up anything in the dog, cat or bird line. *My* constant companions are a small dog, two cats and three canaries. One of the cats and the dog always sleep on my bed at night.

Your affectionate brother,
Edwin H. Dodgson

Writing to his brother Skeffington almost immediately on 20 June 1883, Edwin compared notes about services (MS: Amy Irene Jaques Collection):

Dear Skeff,

Many thanks for your share of your letter – you certainly seem to be always 'on the trot', but though a constant change of home is very unsettling yet it has the advantage of enlarging the experience of places and people. I hope you like your present work but I must say that *I* should immensely prefer having charge of only *one* Church and *one* congregation, and certainly board schools are my *abomination!* I haven't even the 'conscience clause' in my school! I envy you your nearness to Worcester Cathedral and the Malvern Hills. I have been a good deal in that neighbourhood as I have told Isa but I don't know the names of either Suckley or Alfrick. You don't say whether you have daily Service or not but I should [think] that you must find those full Services on the Sunday rather tiring. Last Easter I managed to get the use of another house for the day schools, so that now we really have a *Church*, and not a *school Chapel*. Maggie sent me a lot of her daily text books and I have given a copy to each of the 29 Communicants and I always preach a very short Sermon at the daily Matins on the text for the day and I give an address on the Second Lesson at Evensong, when there is generally a very good congregation. There are not often more than about a dozen at Daily Matins. Every Sunday and Thursday I have an early Celebration with about 24 Communicants every Sunday and 17 on Thursday. Do you have a children's Service in either of your Churches? I have *two* every Sunday during the *long* days (from September to February) and *one* during the rest of the year for the seasons here are just the opposite to the English ones – our shortest day is your *longest*! But the temperature depends almost entirely upon the direction of the winds – the more Northerly from Africa's golden sands the hotter, and the more Southerly from the Antarctic ice the colder. I think you would enjoy the mountain climbing here. Unfortunately my ague-weakened joints forbid me any such indulgences. The top of the mountain is 8500 feet above sea level – it has evidently been a volcano in former ages as there is a large crater at the top now full of water and all the sides for about 4 or 5 thousand feet from the top seemed to be made up of cinders of all sizes. The crater is full of *fresh* water which strange to say rises and falls with the tide! I am now in great hopes that with Charles' help this miserable little settlement may be altogether abandoned very shortly and then I shall be free to return once more into the civilized world! If it wasn't for a good supply of books of different works I think that this isolation and dearth of intellect would drive me mad in a *very* short time. As it is I have continual fits of loneliness and home sickness. I wonder if you will ever pay a visit to Shrewsbury. If so I hope you will call on my late Vicar Smith of All Saints, Castlefields in that town.

Your affectionate brother,

E. H. Dodgson

In 1882, an American ship, the *Henry B Paul*, visited Tristan to ship a cargo of cattle bound for St Helena. She dropped anchor about six miles east of the settlement, but she ran aground on a sand bank, and was left high and dry. In the end she took no cargo, but left Tristan with a legacy that almost brought the island to its knees. The rats on board the stranded ship took flight and reached the island of Tristan, quickly colonising the area and rapidly growing in numbers. Within a short time, they had become a major pest, and the crops of potatoes were seriously affected, being eaten by the large number of rats. This problem, along with other issues, prompted Edwin to believe that the overall solution would be for the islanders to relocate to a new settlement.

Bishop Welby wrote to the SPG in January 1884:

> I have not had an opportunity of hearing from Mr. Dodgson for the last ten months and I see no prospect at present of being able to visit him. I cannot go whaling for an uncertain time with the chance of being landed at Tristan d'Acunha, and then having to wait for a long time until the return of the season in which whalers again touch there to get back to St. Helena …

All did not go well with Edwin. As the years ticked by, Edwin reported that the islanders were as kindly as ever, and he was well provided for in board and lodging. However, he was becoming increasingly despondent about the wayward behaviour of the children, which he attributed to their isolation. In addition, the upsurge in the rat population on Tristan was destroying many of the islanders' crops, and starvation looked imminent.

Some of the young men who had worked with the whalers left the island, realising that life was more exciting in other parts of the world. The population decreased from 107 to 93 within a year or two of Edwin's arrival. There was less unity among the islanders, particularly among some of the older men. One of the men, originally from an American whaler, had begun to monopolise the cattle trade over the course of thirty years, giving him more economic power, which others thought was against the common good. Added to this was the decline in the number of whaling ships calling at Tristan. They had largely moved to new fishing grounds far away from the island. During 1884, only one whaler had been seen in the area.

Edwin reported to the SPG that it had been 'for a long time my daily prayer that God would open some way for us all to leave the island'. A whaling captain reported Edwin's 'very depressed state of mind' to Bishop Welby, but no immediate action was taken.

Charles noted in his diary on 27 September 1883, 'Heard from Edwin, who strongly approves my idea of getting all the Tristan folk moved to the Cape.' So began a series of visits to key people in positions of influence to achieve that end. Here are some entries from Charles's diary that illustrate the efforts he made:

19 October 1883

Went to town by the 9 a.m., to make a beginning in the business about which I heard from Edwin September 27th.

First I called (by appointment) on the Secretary to the Society for the Propagation of the Gospel, the Rev. H. W. Tucker, at 19 Delahay Street, Westminster. He read the copy I had made of parts of Edwin's letter, and agreed in it very decidedly. He was sure the Society would support the proposed move, and, though they could not vote money for secular purposes, he thought they would at least pay the whole £100 grant for the current year in which the move should occur. He approved my idea of going to *see* persons rather than writing, saying that letters 'would only get pigeon-holed', and advised me to apply to the Colonial Office, as the department of the Government who ought to take the initiative in action; and in doing this, to go to a *permanent* under-Secretary rather than the Secretary, Lord Derby. The permanent under-Secretary is Sir R. Herbert,[29] and the assistants the Hon. R. H. Meade,[30] Mr. Bramston[31] and Mr. Wingfield.[32] The only one now in town is Mr. Bramston, with whom I had an interview.

---

[29]   The Rt Hon. Sir Robert George Wyndham Herbert (1831–1905) was permanent under-secretary of state for the colonies from 1871 until 1892.

[30]   The Hon. Sir Robert Henry Meade (1835–1898) was assistant under-secretary in the Colonial Office from 1871 until he became permanent under-secretary of state for the colonies in 1892, a position he held until 1897.

[31]   Sir John Bramston (1832–1921) was assistant under-secretary of state for the colonies from 1876 until 1897.

[32]   Sir Edward Wingfield (1834–1910) was assistant under-secretary of state for the colonies in 1878, and permanent under-secretary from 1897 until 1900.

Mr. Bramston approved my idea of bringing the thing before Mr. Gladstone. He said the Colonial Office could not begin: it was for the Admiralty to send a ship, and the Colonial Office would, if the people could be got to the Cape, interest the Cape authorities in them and get them looked after. He advised my seeing Captain Tryon, the permanent secretary to the Admiralty, to whom I went next.[33] Capt. Tryon discouraged the idea (of Edwin's) that the Government might buy the live stock (valued at from £5,000 to £10,000), as they get their meat by contract, but thought it possible they might ship the people to the Cape as an act of charity. He urged however that I had not the authority needed to act on their behalf (a true bill, I fear, as Edwin has not got their formal consent) and advised letter-writing rather than personal interviews (here I differ). Lastly he thought the Colonial Office was the proper department to take the initiative.

So far I have done little.

20 October 1883

Then to Sir H. Barclay's [sic], at 2 Bina Gardens, South Kensington, but he was out.[34] He is the late Governor at the Cape, and has also been Governor elsewhere, and Mr. Bramston thought he would be able to advise in the Tristan business. Then called at Major Egerton Todd's,[35] and saw him, Mrs. Todd, Ada, and also Maud Fearon, who was calling. Mrs. Todd was much interested in the Tristan affair, and suggested several persons worth applying to, viz. Capt. Mills, head of the Emigration Agency, at 7 Albert Mansions, Victoria Street.[36] His secretary, Mr. Spencer Todd, at 24 Cathcart Road, is Major Todd's brother, and she gave me a note of

---

33  Vice-Admiral Sir George Tryon (1832–1893) was secretary of the Admiralty between 1882 and 1884, appointed rear-admiral in 1884 and vice-admiral in 1889.

34  Sir Henry Barkly (1815–1898) was governor of the Cape of Good Hope from 1870 until he retired on a pension in 1878.

35  Major William Egerton Todd (1831–1896) served in the Indian Mutiny Campaign from 1857 to 1858, achieved the rank of colonel, and retired in 1888.

36  Sir Charles Mills (1825–1895) was a member of the Cape parliament in 1866, permanent under-secretary in 1872, and first agent general in London for Cape Colony in 1882.

introduction to him.[37] Also to Sir Hercules Robinson, the present Governor of the Cape, who is at present in Scotland.[38] Also promised one for Sir Donald Currie (this never came. 4/5/87).[39]

29 October 1883

Went to town, to join the Wilcox party (Margaret, Clara, and Dora), at 12 Margaret Street, Cavendish Square. Left bag there, and went to Office of Colonial Agency (7 Albert Mansions) and saw Mr. Spencer Todd. He dwelt much on the idea of Edwin's people settling at the Cape, and said I should get from Edwin a list of them, with ages (I wrote next day for it): also he thought the *Cape* Government would perhaps send for them, and that the cattle should go *alive*: but they would have to borrow a ship from Home Government.

Thence I went to the Carlton, and saw Sir H. Barclay [*sic*] (late Governor at the Cape). He will see Capt. Mills etc., and talk over the matter.

30 October 1883

Went again to Colonial Agency, and saw Mr. Scanlan [*sic*], Prime Minister at the Cape,[40] and Capt. Mills, the head of the Agency. Mr. Scanlan said the proper course was to apply (myself – or, better,

---

37  (John) Spencer Brydges Todd (1840–1921) was a civil servant who served the Cape of Good Hope from 1860 until 1904, becoming secretary of the department of agent general in London from 1882 until 1904, and executive commissioner for the Cape.

38  Sir Hercules George Robert Robinson (1824–1897), first Baron Rosmead, was governor of Cape Colony and high commissioner of South Africa from 1880 until 1889, a privy councillor in 1882, who returned to South Africa as governor in 1895, retiring from colonial activity in 1897.

39  Sir Donald Currie (1825–1909) was head of Donald Currie & Company, ship owners, but also MP for Perthshire 1880–1885, and MP for West Perthshire 1885–1900.

40  Hon. Sir Thomas Charles Scanlen (1834–1912) was a member in the Cape House of Assembly from 1870 until 1896, JP for the districts of Cape and Cradock, prime minister and attorney general of the Cape Colony in 1881, prime minister and colonial secretary in 1882, appointed legal adviser to the British South Africa Company in 1894, member of the executive council in 1896, member of the legislative council in 1899, and on several occasions he acted as the company's representative, retiring on a pension in 1908.

through Colonial Office) to the Commissioner of Crown Lands and Public Works at the Cape. The matter would then go to the Governor, and so to the Ministers, and if *they* approve, the Governor will apply to the Admiralty to lend a ship.

Capt. Mills added little to this, except to point out that the Cape Government have no jurisdiction at Tristan: so that the Home Government *must begin* the action.

Charles received the following letter from Sir Hercules Robinson dated 2 November 1883 (MS: Dodgson Family):

Dear Sir,

I am generally at home up to 10.30 a.m. and would be happy to see you any morning next week if you wish to call. But before giving you the trouble to do so I think it fair to tell you that I am sure it will not be in my power to do anything for you in the matter to which you refer. The Cape has now Parliamentary Government, and all matters of local concern – such as immigration – are under the control of the responsible Advisers of the Governor. All I could do for you, therefore, would be to refer you to the Premier, Mr. Scanlen, whom I understand you have already interviewed.

If notwithstanding you still wish to see me it will give me much pleasure to receive you.

Faithfully yours,

Hercules Robinson

Charles made the appointment to meet Sir Hercules Robinson.

9 November 1883

At quarter to 10 I had an interview, by appointment, with Sir Hercules Robinson, Governor at the Cape, about 'Tristan'. He discouraged hope, on the ground that the people will probably be discontented, and go back. Still, he thought that, if they petition the Cape Government, and if it appears probable they would settle at the Cape, the Home Government might give them free passage. He agreed with Mr. Scanlan [*sic*] as to petition going *first* to the Commissioner of Crown Lands etc. but differed as to his own application to Home Government. He thought *that* would be to Mr. Gladstone, to whom I shall therefore send details.

Eventually, Charles found an ally in George Smyth Baden Powell (1847–1898), whom he met on 25 November 1883:

> A Mr. Baden Powell (8 St. George's Place, Hyde Park Corner) called to talk about Tristan, having heard what I am doing, and being interested in it. He is at present doing some business for the Colonial Office, and undertook to make out exactly under which Government Department Tristan is. He suggested what seems an excellent idea, that in Australia they are anxious for immigrants (at least in two departments, South Australia, and New South Wales) and would *give* them land. The cost of emigration (assisted) from England is only £6 a head, and it would not be hard to arrange for an emigrant-ship calling there. The only difficulty is getting the cattle there: but these, as he suggested need not be taken further than the Cape (where they would be easily sold at large prices). He knows the Agents General for these departments . . . and will try to arrange for my having interviews with them.

Charles met with Baden Powell again on 30 November to be introduced to the various agents general, but he left with only some pamphlets about New South Wales, and a rebuff that 'they did not want any more emigrants in South Australia'. The Crown agent for New Zealand was too busy to see Charles. Further contact with Baden Powell ceased until March 1887.

Charles went to remarkable lengths to achieve the relocation of the Tristan islanders. He saw many key and influential people in government and in the civil service, yet he met with prevarication, indifference and abdication of responsibility. Undaunted, he continued in his search for a solution. A letter, dated 5 January 1884, that Charles sent to Mrs Egerton Todd (MS: Berol Collection) indicated that the matter was still exercising his mind:

Dear Mrs. Todd,

Many thanks for all the trouble that has been so kindly taken, through unknown friends, to procure an introduction for a letter from me to Sir D. Currie. But I fear I can't write it! It is much too big a business to be put into a *short* letter: and a long one is impossible. I have not yet found time to write the letter about it which Miss Gladstone will put before her father. To Sir D.C. I must state it *viva voce*, if at all. But the Gladstones know him well, so that a first-hand introduction is available … Believe me

Sincerely yours,

C. L. Dodgson

P.S. … I think we *may* manage for Tristan private conveyance to the Cape, and thence *aided* emigration to New South Wales.

There can be no doubt that Charles tried very hard to find a suitable way for the Tristan islanders to find a better home. But the barrier of officialdom and the intricate procedures of the civil service proved hard to penetrate. Hence, Charles shifted his endeavours in an attempt to get Edwin home and replace him for a year with a temporary clergyman.

The next account we have is from a letter that Charles sent to Henry Tucker, secretary of the SPG, dated 8 April 1884 (MS: SPG). The letter began with an extract written by Edwin to his brother explaining his circumstances, dated 9 November 1883:

One of my castles in the air is that, in case no means for a general exodus from the place are possible at present, some self-denying Priest should come out here in the next man-of-war, and take my place for a year: I being then able to get a passage in her to the Cape, and from thence to England, to return here in the *next* man-of-war when my *locum tenens* could depart in the same manner: for every man-of-war, which calls here, goes direct to the Cape, before proceeding to the Australian station.

I would most gladly hand over to him my stipend for that year, and he would be boarded and lodged here freely, as I am. I should think the S.P.G. would be willing to pay my passage home from the

Cape, and probably that of my *locum tenens* also; or they might deduct it out of my stipend, if such payments are not in accordance with their rules: and a passage in a man-of-war could be easily managed, and would cost little or nothing except a few stewards, etc.

Three years' work, followed by one year's rest, is the recognised rule in the C.A.M., though *all* the workers do not take advantage of it.

Of course I would leave all Church materials, and most of my own books and other belongings for the use of the *locum tenens*, so that he would be just as comfortable as I am now.

————

Christ Church, Oxford
April 8, 1884
Dear Sir,

I send you the above extract from a letter of my brother's, in hopes that you may either be able, through the machinery of the S.P.G. to find some clergyman able and willing to go out in the manner proposed, or at least to suggest some way of finding one.

The migration of the population of the island, to the Cape or elsewhere, would be no doubt much facilitated if my brother could come to England and himself plead their cause.

He announces that a plague of rats has begun, which eat up the potatoes, and thus add the prospect of starvation to the other weighty reasons already urged for depopulating the island. Believe me

Very truly yours,
C. L. Dodgson

Tucker replied on 12 April, and Charles followed up the response with the following letter dated 14 May (MS: SPG):

... I don't think we need come to the S.P.G. for any help in money towards sending a *Locum Tenens* to Tristan for a year, so as to let my brother come to England. But what I now write to ask is, if I can find anyone willing to go, and could provide all necessary expenses, would the S.P.G. *authorise* the step, and send him out under their auspices?

Secondly, could you, through the machinery of the S.P.G., enquire for a suitable man? (I know of no way of doing it but by advertising.)

Thirdly, do you think there would be any use in applying to the Government (I should apply to Mr. Gladstone himself, if at all) to *give* such a man his passage in a Man-of-War? Is it a kind of thing they ever do? (A Man-of-War seems to be the only chance, now, for getting to Tristan *at all*: the whalers have quite ceased to run between it and St. Helena) ...

In the meantime, life on Tristan continued with positive and negative events. On the positive side, Edwin performed two weddings, as his letter to his sister Louisa records, dated 29 April 1884. But a shortage of various foods was also exercising Edwin's mind (MS: Amy Irene Jaques Collection):

Dearest Louisa,

My budget to Mary left off with the information that I had two weddings lately – one on Low Sunday and the other the following Tuesday. The one on Sunday was at 10 o'clock in the morning. It was a very hot day and the presence of, I believe, every man, woman and child on the Island did not make the Church particularly cool. We sang two hymns, one before the Service and the other at the end, nos. 351 and 274. I taught two of my Altar Servers to serve at a Marriage, so as to make the Service as impressive as possible, for as a proper Church wedding is of course an unknown thing to *this* generation ... You can easily understand what a reverent sort of Service it must have been for Whaling Captains to scramble the Church Service in a crowded kitchen. After the last hymn I gave the bride and bridegroom a short simple address of my own instead of the somewhat antiquated one in the prayer book, chiefly founded on an address of Walsham How's in *Pastor in Parochial* ... Bride and bridegroom spoke out their vows clearly and as if they meant what they said. The bride was naturally a pretty fair girl with flaxen hair, but on this occasion she and her friends had managed to torture her hair into stiff corkscrew curls, which were of a dusky black colour, and from the general appearance of her hair I should say it had been curled with *tar*. The result was to transform a natural blonde into a hideous caricature of a brunette ...

(5 May 1884) I am taking a half holiday this morning as I felt very weary and dreary after yesterday's Services, so I can have a little quiet time for letter writing which I don't often get. There is one bridal veil on the Island which one of the women wore at her own wedding at St. Helena about 16 years ago and brought here with her. I believe it has done duty at every wedding on the Island ever since that time and as it is of a very flimsy nature I *don't think* it has ever been washed, so you may imagine how nice and fresh it looks now! I couldn't help thinking that if the bride had been dressed in a clean print dress, and with her hair dressed naturally and neatly how *much* nicer she would have looked than in an unnatural state of dirty tawdriness, but of course I said nothing about it and I have no doubt the people thought her looking grand and *ladylike*! Tuesday's bride looked very much better. She has a thoroughly Jewish face with dark skin and black hair and eyes and is altogether the prettiest girl on the Island. She only wore *two* curls – one on each side of her face and as they were *wavy* curls, they only looked as if they had been done up too loosely and had *come down*! The *Sunday's* bride was married with her married sister's ring, which formerly belonged to her deceased mother – Mrs. Hagan, who died last year, and the *Tuesday's* bride had a ring of *her own* which belongs to her deceased grandmother – old Mrs. Swain, and has never been used since her death about 12 years ago. So you see how rings are handed down here from generation to generation ... After the Service on Sunday the wedding party adjourned to Captain Hagan's house when the signing was done, for about a year before I came, a Man of War brought a marriage register here which has now come into use for the first time. I then shook hands with the Bride and Bridegroom and went back to the Church to get ready for Mattins, as it was just time for it. On Monday at about one o'clock the wedding dinner took place which included everybody on the Island in two or three relays. Of course I had to preside and a very bountiful dinner it was. I believe that two sheep were slaughtered for the occasion, and about a dozen sucking pigs, to say nothing of geese and fowls and for the

second course were 13 large plain suet puddings and sundry tarts, but I am thankful to say that the universal drink was *water* with a small jug of milk for *my* special benefit. I don't think there is a drop of wine or spirits on the Island now except the Communion wine . . . They cheered the Bride heartily, but when it came to *singing* 'For he's a jolly good fellow', it appeared that nobody had ever heard it, so it was almost a solo on my part, till I came to the three cheers at the end which they gave most lustily and afterwards one cheer more for the Bride *and* Bridegroom. We repeated the same ceremony when all the others had finished dining and they asked me to come back into the house and *lead* them, which I did and *this* time the health song was much more hearty. After this was all over, what with the heat and the noise, I was fit for nothing but perfect quiet and rest with my head like a red hot cannon ball, so that I had a very good excuse for not attending the wedding dance party in the evening, which I was very glad to be able to get out of without hurting anybody's feelings, particularly as I had another wedding to take on the following day. The Tuesday wedding was fixed for 8 a.m. and as both Bride and Bridegroom have been regular Communicants for a long time the Service concluded with a Celebration as ought always to be the case. The order of the Marriage Service was exactly the same as on the Sunday and in 2 or 3 hours after the signing was done we had *another* wedding dinner for the whole Island, and it was as nearly as possible a facsimile of the one on Monday with one exception. As I said on Saturday that a wedding cake ought to contain a ring and a three-penny bit, so that the person who got the ring would be the next bride – *if eligible*, and the unfortunate possessor of the 3*d*. would be doomed to celibacy, so on Monday morning one of the children was sent to me to request the two necessary articles, which I furnished, a small picture ring coming in very handy for the occasion. When the cake was cut on Tuesday the children were very anxious that *I* should get the ring. I told them that if I did I should throw it over my shoulder amongst the girls behind me and they might scramble for it, but unfortunately the ring and the money fell to the lot of middle aged married women with large families! We sang the Bridegroom's health twice on the Tuesday as before, but on that day the song was *by no means* a solo. I believe the young people had been practising it among themselves and ever since that day I am constantly hearing it sung about the place with variations. *Again* I was able to furnish a most excellent excuse for my absence from the dancing at night, not that I have the slightest objection to the people enjoying themselves in that way to their heart's content but oh *the heat! – the crush!* and *the noise!* I have made a point of attending a sufficient number of dance parties to let the people clearly see that they have my entire approval, so now I think that I may absent myself with a clear conscience, and I have no doubt that my room is preferable to my company! As it happens I have always lately had an extra severe headache on such occasions, so for all the people know I may be *longing* to be present if well enough! I meant to have begun school again after the holidays on the Thursday before Low Sunday but in honour of the two weddings I gave the children another week or rather more till the following Monday week. My head was so *fearfully* bad on the Wednesday after the wedding that I lay in bed all day in a comatose condition, and I felt very weak for some days afterwards. I wonder if my head will *ever* get into tolerable order again. I believe what I really want is to be *fed up*, and if ever I am allowed to come back to England, I think I must have a good spell of it before I shall be fit for harness again. During the last week another of the lapsed communicants threw away his share of the Sunday flow[?][41] and signed the same sort of paper which the other man had done a fortnight before. I read it in Church last Sunday and he will return to H.C. [Holy Communion] on Sunday next – he has also chosen a special act of self punishment and I feel sure he is most truly penitent. I do believe that this sad falling away of Communicants will prove to be a real blessing to themselves, and to the rest of the people, by making them think of sin much more as a *reality*, which *must* be a good thing for them. I have just taught the children a new hymn for the children's service – No. 330 'I love to hear the Story' – it is one of the simplest hymns in A. & M., and it goes capitally to a pretty easy tune which Mr. Gray of Helmsley picked up somewhere. I thought perhaps Mary might like to have it for the Southwick children's service so I will put down the notes as

---

[41]  The word is unreadable – possibly 'flow' or 'flour', making the full meaning difficult to determine. If 'flow' it could perhaps refer to Communion wine, or 'flour' could mean Communion bread.

well as I can by ear without an instrument. When you play it over you will easily see any mistakes.

m  | m$^1$ | m  | m$^1$ r m | s$^1$  | f$^1$
m  | m$^1$ | m  | m$^1$ f m | r$^1$  | ..$^1$ chorus
m  | m$^1$ | m  | m$^1$ r m | s$^1$  | f
m  | m$^1$ | m  | r$^1$ m r  | d$^1$ | ..$^1$
s  | s$^1$ | s  | s$^1$ l t  | d$^1$ | r$^1$
d  | d$^1$ | t  | l$^1$ t l  | s$^1$ | ..$^1$
s  | s$^1$ | s  | s$^1$ l t  | d$^1$ | r$^1$
d  | d$^1$ | t  | l$^1$ t l  | s$^1$ | ..$^1$

(chorus repeated)

I have marked the accented notes, and the double accent on the 'doh' and 'ray' in the 5th and 7th lines shew that they [?] on the *upper* 'doh' and 'ray' as well as the 'dohs' in the lines 6 and 8. By singing it in the key of D the highest note 'r$^1$' will of course be E which is about high enough for school children. One of the musical geniuses can easily transpose the tonic sol fa notes into the ordinary playing notation. It is in ¾ time. I have marked the bars and the accented notes have 2 beats except when there are three notes in a bar and then they are all of equal time. You will see it goes with a capital *swing*. Perhaps you may know it, but I don't think I have even seen it written down. The slurs of course show 2 notes to one syllable. Then I think you ought to be able to make it out *now*! It *must* not be sung too fast or it will sound like a jig! We always sing 'Hark the sound of holy voices' to the tune of 'Daily daily sing the praises', for my voice has got so strained now with weakness and the effect of a severe cold on my chest two years ago that I try as far as I can to reserve my singing powers for the Services themselves and that I can only *just* manage now, but I do my best, and as we have always had the *same* chants to the Canticles ever since I came, the people can and do chant them without any need of my help except in starting them. All the services are still very well attended – even the daily Mattins generally has a very fair congregation. Only *once* since I began the daily Services have we ever had a plain read Service and that was one day last year in the middle of the influenza epidemic and when I had a bad cold on my chest, and it was all I could do even to *read* the Service. By the bye I heard the other day that Captain Cleghorne, the only whaling captain who came here from St. Helena last season, told one of the men that there were six cases waiting for me there, and one of them was a harmonium. Whether that is only a guess on his part I know not. Certainly I should have been very glad of one to play on as the S.P.G. one entirely struck work long ago and has been converted into a door and a chair, as it was utterly useless in its former broken condition. It is just about thirteen months now since the *Sapphire* called here, which was my last medium for information from the civilised world.

11/8/84 I find I have a bit of music paper so I have copied the tune out again, so now I think by correcting one notation by the other and the other by the one you may arrive at a fair impression of the air I mean to convey. I have got through all my Services today with the usual red-hot cannon-ballish result to my head, so after having had a little rest I think I cannot do better than finish off this budget, which is my nearest possible approach to talking, which I believe would do me more good than anything else. Oh what wouldn't I give for even an hour's ordinary conversation with some *intelligent* being!

That poor little baby which was born about two months ago with an abscess on its back is still alive though it is nothing now but skin and bone. It takes very little nourishment and seems to have no strength to cry on for more, but it doesn't appear to suffer any pain as it quietly lingers on from day to day. It was asleep yesterday morning at the time when it is usually washed and it never woke till after dark in the evening. It will be a happy day for the child and a great relief to its mother when it is taken Home, but there must be some good reason beyond our understanding for it being allowed to live on in this way. It is a strange thing that ever since that Sunday trade the men have not got a single ship to trade with though generally April is about the best month for ships in the year. The result is that we have now entered upon winter with very little chance of any ships for the next 3 or 4 months with no tea, coffee, or sugar on the Island, and *very* little flour, so I fully expect to have to live on potatoes, water, and a little salt meat, for milk is getting very scarce and I abominate salt butter and have a special dislike to salt meat. I find now that I shall be able to keep on a weekly Celebration of H.C. till about the end of August if necessary, but what will happen after that God only knows, and it is a great comfort to feel that in this matter *I* can do absolutely *nothing*. The wine is most probably waiting at St. Helena and *I* can do nothing towards getting it brought over. You can't think what a hard trial of patience it is to be *longing* to hear news of all kinds – domestic – Church and mission and month after month to go by without bringing any, and of course nobody here can the least enter into my feelings, and it is really amusing to see their ... surprise at my wishing so much for letters and newspapers! There is one sore in this my bundle of thorns and that is that if ever I *do* get into the world again what a lot of newspaper reading I shall have to revel in! I suspect there must be a good many *Guardian*s and other newspapers for me at St. Helena and also a year's *Church Times* which Lambeth always sends me. There have been two big rats in my room this evening – one of the cats has killed one of them and *Sailor* has just killed the other. Does *Clover* ever make himself of use in that way? I don't suppose I shall have a chance of sending this letter off for some 3 or 4 months so it will be well seasoned if ever it reaches you! Best love to all.

Yours very affectionate brother,

E. H. Dodgson

Edwin kept an exercise book containing essays written by some of his school pupils. They mainly repeated each other, and their use of English was restricted (not corrected here). Edwin tried to get them to record in their own words some of the major events that had happened over the years on Tristan. Here are a couple of examples. The first was written by Frederick B Green (MS: Amy Irene Jaques Collection):

The *Mabel Clark* a American merchantman ran ashore on Tristan d'Acunha May year 1878, and there were twenty men on board and six of them got lost. The Captain and his wife and his daughter, and it was very rough and some of the men swam ashore and some of them wait till the next day and the boat come off and bring them ashore. The *Mabel Clark* came from Liverpool going to Hong Kong.

The *Edward Vittery* ran ashore on Tristan d'Acunha and Mr. Dodgson came in the *Edward Vittery* and most all his things got lost.

This report from Amy Matilda Green indicates the kind of food that the children were able to collect on the island:

> Sometimes our men and boys go off in a boat to catch fish and crayfish, mackerel and clipfish, congers and blue fish and snook and soldiers – sometimes they catch plenty of fish and sometimes they catch none. Sometimes our men and boys and girls go round the bluff to get penguin eggs – when its low water they cross the bluff and when it's high water they cross the hill. Sometimes our men and boys catch birds – sometimes our boys and men go on the hill to get night birds eggs, and black eaglet eggs. Sometimes our boys and men and women and girls go down on the rocks and catch crayfish – we fish long lines and hooks – we get night birds eggs out of a long hole – we get two eggs out of a hole, and sometimes our men and boys go down Sandy Point to get black eaglets. Some of the birds names are Kingbirds, 'Pee-oh', sea hens and stinkers, thrush and Island cock, mud bird and Mother Carey chickens, skipjack, petrel.

*Tristan islanders building a boat*

And finally this report from Robert F Glass gives a general view of life on the island:

> We get our flour from the whalers. We grow cabbage. We grow potatoes. We have to build our houses out of soft stones. We thatch our houses with tussock. We get our cloth from the ships. We had a gale once and it blew down one lamb house, and it blew down one hut. We had two cows fall over bank. We get our sugar from the ships. We have got donkeys. We have sheep. We have bullocks. We have cows. We have plenty of rats. We got pigs. We got geese. We got fowls, and we got dogs. We get our molasses from the whalers. We get our cocoa from the men of war. We got a woman on the Island weigh two hundred and fifty, and her name is Eliza. We have to get guano to dress our ground to make the potatoes. I went one day on big ridge and got twenty four birds. We chase a Italian ship out of sight of the Island and the Captain, Mate and sailors. The Captain was just like Billy Hagan. Old Jack and the mate was just like Carlo, and the sailors was just like sheep. I got a pair of bullocks name 'orange' and 'blue'.

The Admiralty asked the island's leader, Peter Green, to write a report for them, stating the current situation on Tristan. His letter, dated January 1885, contained details of the growing disagreements between the elders, and a difference of opinion with Edwin Dodgson. These extracts give his personal feelings about the causes:

> Mr. Dodgson says we have a strange dislike to killing cattle or sheep for our own eating. Now I will give you the reason for it. A certain man has by his mean action come in the possession of nearly half of the cattle on the island, likewise the pasture; he found the pasture; the pasture was the labour of the English pioneers. There was only a small portion of the land cleared when I was wrecked; I had to clear my share. Now this man came after all the land was ready for cattle; now he can kill, sell, and have plenty left.
>
> The Rev. E. H. Dodgson is going to break up this settlement. He has made up the account of our cattle, sheep, donkeys, fowls, etc. He

made the cattle to amount to 500, sheep 500; that is far below the mark … I have been here over 48 years, my wife has been on the island over 57 years. We have not everything we want, but is it not the same in England? So we must take the good times and the bad times.

Can the Rev. E. H. Dodgson take our people away without the consent of the Government, or the Admiralty to have something to say about it?

Peter Green was clearly reluctant to vacate the island, and was not in favour of relocation for all the inhabitants. He was in favour of some people leaving the island, but pointed out the importance of keeping the place sufficiently populated for the assistance of shipping in the area. These matters were expressed in further extracts from his report:

If Mr. Dodgson can get some of our people away from Tristan, I hope he will include the three whaling-boys. One is an American, the other two are natives of Tristan, but they have spent the best part of their lives in whale-ships. They have brought a very small stock of knowledge back to Tristan, and that is of a very vulgar kind.

In three weeks – January 1885 – we boarded six English ships; they all wanted refreshments badly … Sometimes the passing ships have sick people on board; then we come in the shape of doctor. Since 1870 we have had five shipwrecks on Tristan, two at Inaccessible, one at Gough's Island, all a total loss. We received several ship's crews from ships abandoned at sea, so if I may suggest, I should think it necessary to have a good boat's crew at Tristan …

Whether Edwin was aware of Peter Green's opinions is hard to ascertain. However, it did not deter him from planning his return to England to plead the cause of the islanders.

At the end of 1884, the man-of-war HMS *Opal* arrived at Tristan, and Captain Arthur T Brooke took a tour of the island. He met Peter Green, then aged seventy-seven years, and described him as most intelligent and looked upon as the father of the community. He also met Edwin and discussed the idea of relocation with him. Captain Brooke reported that he was convinced that Edwin had done much good for the community, and his ministrations were greatly appreciated by the people. However, he was certain that Edwin was depressed and suffering in health and wanted to leave Tristan. Captain Brooke offered to take him to the Cape, from where he would be able to get back to England. Edwin accepted the offer, but spent the day settling matters before his departure. On the evening of 29 December 1884, Edwin came on board the *Opal* to begin his journey home.

But the journey was not without incident. Edwin accidentally suffered a fall down an open hatchway during a violent storm and was nearly killed. He needed urgent medical treatment on his arrival in London. It transpired that Edwin had seriously damaged his spinal cord.

A letter appeared in the *Times* some years later giving an account of Edwin's departure from the island, written by Admiral Ronald A Hopwood, who had been a midshipman on HMS *Opal* at the time:

> Sir, I was much interested in your article on Tristan da Cunha this morning. I well remember embarking the Rev. E. H. Dodgson about Christmas, 1884, in *H.M.S. Opal*, in which I was then serving as a midshipman.
>
> We were on our way from Cape Coast Castle to Cape of Good Hope, and arrived at Tristan da Cunha on a Saturday, and Mr. Dodgson asked our captain, Arthur Brooke, if he could wait over Sunday to enable him to hold a farewell service, a request which was readily granted. On Sunday, however, it came on to blow so hard that we spent the next few days for the most part under close-reefed topsails. When at length we were able to approach the island there was still too much sea to allow Mr. Dodgson's boat to come alongside, and he was accordingly hoisted in by means of a bo'sun's chair and a whip from the main yard arm!
>
> We landed him at the cape on our way to Australia, and though he was not a very good sailor he earned our gratitude and admiration by most gallantly coming up to take the service on his last Sunday on board, though I fear he was ill repaid by the collapse of his temporary pulpit in a particularly heavy roll, though fortunately not till after he had concluded his sermon.

The boat which you mention as having been swamped with such serious loss of life was, I believe, the one which we took to the island on the same occasion.

Believe me, Sir, yours truly,

Ronald A. Hopwood

Edwin's sister Elizabeth wrote to the SPG on 5 February announcing his arrival back in England, but pointing out his serious condition (MS: SPG):

Dear Sir,

We have just had a glad surprise in the return of our brother from Tristan d'Acunha. We did not know till Tuesday evening that he had even left Tristan, and he arrived yesterday evening. He seems very well except that he is suffering a good deal from the effects of a bad fall on his head while on board the ship 'Spartan' on its way to Southampton. He is ordered to keep perfectly quiet, so cannot write himself, but he seems decidedly better today. He wishes you to be told that he drew £60 for his passage money, and as soon as he can means to write to you and explain all about it and put it right. I remain dear Sir,

Yours truly,

E. L. Dodgson

Charles noted in his diary:

9 February 1885

Edwin is at Guildford, but I have not been to see him yet, as he had a bad fall on the ship, and struck his head, causing concussion, and is ordered rest and silence.

Now back home with his family, Edwin sought help from his brother Charles to lobby the government again to move the islanders. Once Edwin had sufficiently recovered, Charles recommenced the task, but instead of approaching civil service administrators, he turned to the politicians, using contacts that he had already established. Charles was already well acquainted with Robert Arthur Talbot Gascoyne-Cecil

(1830–1903), third Marquess of Salisbury, a Christ Church man and chancellor of Oxford University from 1869. Charles was known to Lord Salisbury and his family, and had been a house-guest at the family seat, Hatfield House in Hertfordshire, on a number of occasions. Lord Salisbury was currently Prime Minister and Foreign Secretary and well-placed to help. Charles wrote to him on 12 December 1885 (MS: Hatfield) opening the discussion on the fate of the Tristan islanders.

Dear Lord Salisbury,

I have been waiting for the Election-storm to blow over, before venturing to trouble you with a matter, which however I think important enough to ask your attention to now. When you have read this letter, you will, I hope, think that I had sufficient grounds for so doing.

The Island of Tristan d'Acunha has about 100 inhabitants, and my brother, the Rev. Edwin H. Dodgson, has been for about 4 years 'priest in charge', under the Bishop of St. Helena. The people were thriving enough, so long as whalers came that way, who were good customers for fresh meat and vegetables. But the whales have deserted those seas, and no ship comes near them, and, to crown all, the island is now swarming with rats, who eat all the crops. The people are on the verge of starvation, and it is a matter of urgency that some steps should be taken *at once*, to remove them to the Cape, or Australia, or somewhere they can live. My brother is now in England, in hopes of getting something done, and (to come to the point) what I have to ask is that you will be so very kind as to let him come to you and tell you about it. Then you will be able to say what should be done, and would be all-powerful in *getting* it done.

I have myself spoken to many officials on the subject, as for instance Captain Tryon at the Admiralty, and Secretary at the Colonial, Sir Hercules Robinson, also the Cape Premier, also the Government Agent for New Zealand, etc., etc., but I believe one talk with you *yourself* would be of more service than anything *I* have been able to do.

My brother would be able to call on you any day after the 21st.

Always sincerely yours,

C. L. Dodgson

Lord Salisbury responded on 15 December (MS copy: Hatfield):

Dear Mr. Dodgson,
The case you mention is a very hard one, I do not think, however, that anything could be done without considerable previous arrangement, and no good purpose would be served by our entering into such arrangements unless there was a probability of our continuing in office long enough to complete them. It is evident that these people could not be moved to the mainland without first preparing for them some species of occupation or means of livelihood which would prevent them being a burden upon the Colony; in fact I believe the Colonies would decline to receive them. I shall not be in London after the 21st until some days after the New Year, but if your brother still wishes me to see him I shall be happy to do so. At the same time I repeat that I think the matter had better be deferred for a few weeks.

Charles followed it up with this letter dated 20 December 1885 (MS: Hatfield):

Dear Lord Salisbury,
It was most kind of you, in the midst of all your business, to answer my letter so fully. Two things more I might as well have mentioned (I was trying to be *very* brief, and it was a case of *obscurus fio*) which would have prevented your thinking that the Tristan people would appear (at the Cape or elsewhere) as *paupers*, and that the Colonies would decline to receive them. One is, that they have a large amount of cattle and other live stock, which, if it could be got *alive* to the Cape, would at once sell for at least £10,000 – probably more: the other, that New South Wales would be very glad to have them, and that Sir Saul Samuel (the Government Agent) said 'whenever you can let me know that you can get these people conveyed to the Cape, I will at once arrange that an emigrant-ship shall call for them and they can be taken to Australia for about £4 a head.'[42]

---

[42] The Hon. Sir Saul Samuel (1820–1900) was a member of the legislative assembly and legislative council from 1854 until 1880, colonial treasurer and postmaster general of New South Wales from 1859 until 1880, and agent general for New South Wales in England from 1880 until 1897.

I expect to see my brother in a day or two, and, if he still wishes to see you *at once*, I will write to ascertain what time would suit you. He could of course call at Hatfield if you would see him there, as he is only an hour from London. Believe me always

Very truly yours,

C. L. Dodgson

On 30 December 1885 Charles recorded in his diary:

To town for the day ... In afternoon Edwin joined me, and we called on Lord Salisbury at Foreign Office, and had a talk (not very fruitful, I fear) on 'Tristan d'Acunha'. However, it may have done good simply to bring Edwin into personal relations with him.

After this meeting, Lord Salisbury gave further consideration to the plight of the Tristan islanders, and wrote back to Charles on 4 January 1886 (MS copy: Hatfield):

Dear Mr. Dodgson,

Since I had the pleasure of seeing you at the Foreign Office, I have made enquiries with respect to Tristan d'Acunha. I am informed that it does not lie in the ordinary track of vessels going to Australia, and that the danger of sending a vessel there is so considerable that the Admiralty avoid doing so except in case of manifest necessity. They further informed me that the Commander on the West Coast of Africa was instructed some time ago that the next vessel which called at the Island was to take a large quantity of rat poison to be exchanged to the islanders for supplies. I fear that your idea of arranging the exportation of the islanders, together with their cattle, on board Her Majesty's ships, is entirely impracticable. The expense of doing so would be very great, especially in consideration of the very bad landing there is at the island; and it is doubtful whether the cattle would, when they arrived in South Africa, fetch the money which they would cost to bring. On the other hand, the Colonial Authorities resist the importation of immigrants wholly destitute of means. But there is the far larger and far graver difficulty beyond all these, that if the Government consented to undertake the transportation of this body of immigrants from Tristan d'Acunha to the Cape, they could hardly refuse to do it in other cases nearer home; and there are, both in England and in Ireland great numbers of people who would gladly get across to the opposite side of the Atlantic if they had only the means of doing so. The Government has always refused to undertake this duty, as too onerous for the public purse, and as one belonging more properly to private enterprise; and I am afraid there is no chance of their relaxing the rule in this one particular instance.

Yours very truly,

Salisbury

Back on Tristan, tragedy had struck the islanders. On 27 November 1885, fifteen men had rowed out in an attempt to intercept the ship *West Riding* to trade for provisions to help feed the inhabitants of Tristan. Accounts suggest that they rowed out in rough seas, their boat capsized, and they were all drowned. They were certainly never seen again. This left very few adult men on the island.[43]

The captain of the *West Riding* was William Thomas, and he was on his way to Australia. Captain Thomas's account of this tragic incident was published in a Sydney newspaper on 13 January 1886:

On November 27th, at 4 a.m., saw the Island of Tristan da Cunha, S.E. by S. true, there being at the time strong squalls with a heavy sea, though the weather was clear. The settlement on the island bore S.W. distant nine miles, and a large fire was observed on shore in the vicinity.

Soon afterwards a sailing boat was sighted steering for the vessel, being then distant about six miles from the settlement. Captain Thomas immediately took in sail, and had his ship brought to the wind on the port

---

[43]  The twelve married men who drowned were Thomas Cotton, Joseph Beetham, William Green, Thomas Swayne, Samuel Swayne, Jacob Green, William Hagan, Jeremiah Green, Cornelius Cotton, John Green, Thomas Glass and William Peter Green. The three unmarried men were Fred Green, Albert Hagan and Steven Hagan. This left three married men on the island: old Peter Green, Captain Hagan and Samuel Hagan, together with five unmarried men/boys: Henry Green, Andrew Hagan, Joseph Glass, Andrew Swayne and Joshua Rogers.

tack. At 7.40 when the boat was on the barque's port quarter, distant one and a half miles, its sailing mast suddenly disappeared. The boat was afterwards seen, apparently making towards the vessel with paddles. Thinking some accident had happened, Captain Thomas made sail, and stood towards the supposed spot where the boat was first seen; but although the ship cruised in the vicinity for two hours with the captain and mate in the mizzentop with telescopes, she failed to discover any vestige of it or its occupants. As the wind was from S.W. and the vessel was rolling dreadfully, broadside on to the sea, having a heavy cargo on board, and there being a north-easterly current and a heavy sea, it was found impossible to communicate with the island, Captain Thomas not deeming it prudent to launch a boat, at 10 a.m.; believing that nothing more could be done to assist anyone, Captain Thomas kept the vessel away on her course. Seeing that the inhabitants were so eager to communicate, during the prevalence of strong winds and a heavy sea, in a small boat, with a vessel nine or ten miles direct to leeward of the settlement, it is conjectured that some shipwrecked people have probably got ashore on the island.

The truth was that all lives in the boat heading for the *West Riding* were lost. Life thereafter was a real struggle for the islanders without the strength of the men to assist in the day-to-day activities that made living on Tristan a viable proposition. Hearing of this desperate loss some months later, Edwin immediately wrote to the Admiralty. His letter, dated 4 March 1886, said:

> When I left that island in December 1884, the rats were beginning to do such serious damage to the potatoes, the main support of the inhabitants, that it seemed to me that unless some means could be devised for transporting the people to some other place they must inevitably sooner or later be reduced to starvation. From various causes I have not yet been able to make such arrangement ... I fear that the people must be already in great straits, for under ordinary circumstances they would have regarded it as an act of madness to attempt to board a vessel nine miles to leeward in such dangerous weather.

I now write to request your Lordship most earnestly to arrange for one of Her Majesty's ships to visit the island and ascertain its present condition as soon as possible.

Although this strengthened Edwin's argument for relocation, it was not unanimously favoured by the islanders. The Admiralty received the following letter from Peter Green a few days later, although it was written on the day following the tragedy:

... A ship came to Tristan. She could not fetch up to the settlement. When she got in shore she was about three miles from us to the eastward. Our life-boat went off to her with sheep, potatoes, geese, etc. When the boat got near the ship she hove aback; the boat was alongside the ship some time, then the ship stood out from the land. We could see our life-boat towing astern to the ship. She stood out about four miles. When she came in again she got so far to the eastward that she was lost to our view. We were watching for the boat all that night, but no boat made her appearance.

Next morning two parties went round the island by land. They could see nothing of the boat. The wind was moderate, the sea was moderate ... One thing is certain; she never reached the island. She had all our best boatmen in her, rather too many, 15 in number, 10 of them married. If the boat and crew is lost it will make Tristan an island of widows ... But I am still in hopes that the boat's crew is still on board the ship. I have lost boats alongside of a ship myself, but the captain of the ship gave us a little boat to go ashore.

Our minister the Rev. E. H. Dodgson left us in H.M.S. *Opal*; he was going to break up this settlement. If the boat's crew is lost it will be broken up with a vengeance.

The Admiralty sent copies of Edwin's letter and Peter Green's letter to the Colonial Office, adding that HMS *Thalia* would probably leave England at the end of April and would be ordered to call at Tristan da Cunha, and if necessary she could convey the inhabitants to the Cape.

The Colonial Office telegraphed the government of the Cape to ask for their assistance. The response they received was lukewarm, indicating that they could offer temporary accommodation, but any expenditure would have to be reimbursed. The Cape ministers added that they were 'unable to give practical expression to their sympathy with the misfortunes of persons living in another country. The number of persons out of employment in the Colony is so great that the chance of fresh arrivals obtaining a livelihood by work is hopeless.' After much negotiation, the Colonial Office changed its plan and drew a sum of £100 from the Civil Contingencies Fund to purchase meal, seed, corn, potatoes and a quantity of rat poison, to be sent out with HMS *Thalia*.

Further disturbing news arrived in the middle of April 1886, some in letters sent by the islanders to Edwin, and some from a report dated 26 December 1885, written by the master of the Glasgow ship *City of Sparta*, A R Johnston, which found its way to the Board of Trade. Johnston wrote that:

> Fifteen of the settlers pulled off to what was supposed an English ship, but neither the 15 of the crew nor their boat ever returned. The settlers watching from the island affirm they saw the boat going alongside the ship, but could not discern her leaving, as the ship was then slowly reaching beyond their vision. They soon afterwards observed the ship dipping her flags (intimating adieu), and then watched and waited eagerly and anxiously for the return of their companions, but nothing had been seen or heard of them since.
>
> The weather at the time was clear with a smooth sea, and a moderate breeze from the southward. Another boat from the island, with seven of a crew, boarded either a German or Norwegian barque on the same day, but they returned safely enough.
>
> The boat the missing men had with them was what they called a whale life-boat, a very valuable and serviceable boat, which was presented to the islanders a year ago by the Board of Trade for rescuing from Inaccessible Island the crew of the British ship *Shakespeare*, which had been wrecked there. Their only remaining boat, which was serviceable only in fine weather, is very shaky and leaky.
>
> The remaining settlers evince serious apprehensions concerning the fate of their missing companions, and are firmly impressed with

the belief that they had no desire to leave the island, unless, as they surmised, the ship referred to was shorthanded and wanted assistance, and that they had volunteered to proceed with this ship to some port. This surmise I think to be very improbable, inasmuch that a ship could hardly want 15 of a crew; and another thing the islanders could hardly be so inhuman as to leave their wives and families in anxiety and misery and wholly unprovided for without first communicating with them. Twelve of the 15 were elderly married men, leaving wives and large families, the remaining were three single boys.

The Colonial Office considered the various accounts of the disaster and came to the conclusion that there was fault on both sides: the callousness of the crew of the *West Riding*, and the carelessness exhibited by the boat of islanders. It offered this explanation. The captain of the *West Riding*, seeing a boat crowded with men approaching his ship, took in sail and hove to, but did not allow them to board. The boat remained alongside for some time, hoping to trade with the ship, but eventually gave up after following the ship for about four miles. By this time they were too leeward of the island and could not pull against the north-easterly current, being driven further and further away. The captain of the *West Riding*, not fully aware of the dreadful consequence of his heartless action, mockingly signalled 'Good-bye'. Finally, realising the precarious situation of the boat, he tried to sight her again, but in vain.

Edwin now contacted the Colonial Office and offered to return, saying, 'I think it is my plain duty to throw in my lot with them and minister to their souls.' The Colonial Office informed him that the Treasury was willing to pay for his passage, and had granted £100 towards provisions.

Edwin suggested that priority should be given to potatoes and flour, but also thought that dresses and underclothing should be sent out, as the women and children were in great need of such items. He thought it would be useless to send seed potatoes and corn, and, for that matter, rat poison. He argued that as the whole island was infested with rats, the task of trying to poison them off would be hopeless, and unless that was done it would be pointless to plant new crops. He also thought that an immense number of decaying bodies of rats on the island would be unhealthy for the inhabitants. Since there were currently only five able-bodied men on Tristan, carrying out the work of destroying the rats would detract from their other important duties. What they needed was food to eat immediately.

Edwin also said that he was anxious to know whether the government had formed any definite plan for the removal of the islanders and their cattle, and, if so, to what place they thought it best to relocate them, and how soon.

A week later, Edwin wrote again to the Colonial Office, restating his view that relocation was the best solution for the Tristanians (the name given by the islanders themselves). The supplies being sent would only bring temporary relief, and there was a danger that in the long term the islanders would starve.

At the end of May, Edwin sailed from Devonport on HMS *Thalia* with the stores provided by the British government. These included clothes, flour and other supplies to the value of £30. Notwithstanding Edwin's advice, they sent seed potatoes and rat poison, and also included some terriers and mongooses, altogether to the value of £70.

The ship arrived back at Tristan on 5 August 1886. The inhabitants were clearly very pleased to have Edwin back. It must have been strange to know that fifteen of the men had been lost at sea, and that many of the women were now widows. Edwin gave what support he could, and the islanders were grateful to someone who knew them well and whose sympathy was heartfelt.

Edwin wrote the following letter for his family back home (quoted in *Historical Sketches, Colonial Series*, no. V, *St Helena and Tristan D'Acunha* (London: SPG, 1901, pp. 17–18):

> It seems both strange and natural to date my letters again from this place. I hadn't any time to write before the *Thalia* left for the Cape, so only added a few lines in pencil to the letter I had begun writing before we got here; so now for the full particulars.

On Tuesday (August 3) it was such rough weather that the captain didn't dare 'make' the island, so we lay-to most of the day; but on Wednesday the weather so moderated that we steamed straight for the island, which we sighted early in the afternoon, and at about 4 o'clock we were within three miles of the shore, and could see the houses, cattle, etc., quite plainly. Captain Bosanquet decided to stand off for the night, so at about nine o'clock on Thursday morning one of the big boats was lowered to go and see whether it was possible for the smaller boats to land, for we could see a considerable surf on the beach. We saw the cutter anchored apparently within 50 yards of the beach, and a lot of people flocking down to the shore, so Captain Bosanquet ordered one of the small whale-boats to be lowered to go and try to land. He gave me leave to go in her, but when we were within 100 yards of the beach we were recalled by signal to the ship. As we rowed back I saw the islanders launch one of their boats and pull off towards the ship. When we got alongside, we found a boat being loaded at each gangway, so were ordered to lie off and wait. In the meantime the island boat went alongside and Peter Green got on board; and the boat, containing Captain Hagan and four or five of the young men came alongside of us, so that I could shake hands with them all, and enter upon a storm of questions and answers. They all seemed intensely delighted at seeing me once more, and hearing that I was willing to stop with them again. I am delighted to find that my elder schoolboys, who have been forced into manhood by the loss of their fathers, have turned out far more manly than I ever expected; they are really now such nice young fellows, and quite conversational.

When I landed on the beach I had my hands nearly shaken off by the women and girls, who all came running down on the first tidings of my coming. They said no conventional words of welcome, but the warm grasp of their hands and their beaming faces showed their real feelings. The only special words of welcome that I remember were spoken by old Mrs. Green, when she shook hands with me, and she evidently meant them – 'God bless, you, sir, for coming to us!' After all the stores were landed I bade farewell to the officers and men who brought them, and then was conducted up to the houses in a sort of triumphal procession. I have got my old quarters again, with the same furniture, etc., and I am writing this letter with the ink I left in one of my bottles when I came away more than a year and a half ago! They have never received any letter from me, so had made up their minds I must be dead. They tell me that they have often said, since the boat was lost, that if only I would come back it wouldn't be so lonely. They had boarded an English ship about a week before I came, which told them that the boat's crew had never been picked up, so I was spared the pain of having to take away their last hope. Poor people! They feel their loss terribly, and it *does* seem so strange to miss so many familiar faces. There have been no deaths here since I went, except those fifteen men, but five more babies have arrived, whom I am going to baptize next Sunday. Rachel Green, the young widow to whom you sent the wedding dress, etc., has a little girl to be baptized, and I have agreed to be her godfather, as poor Rachel evidently wished it very much, and her husband and I were special friends – he *was* such a nice young fellow – a regular communicant, and so earnest and simple-minded in religion.

August 10. I have had a very busy day today; all the morning, and up to about 2 this afternoon, I was engaged in serving out the print, flannel, etc.; and then at 4 p.m. we had a meeting of all heads of the different families to settle plans for the future in regard to church, school, and my own board, etc. I also took the opportunity of ascertaining the amount of stock, etc., every one possessed, and find that altogether there are on the island 536 cattle of all sorts, 656 sheep, and 42 donkeys. These are all most unequally divided, *e.g.* one family has 94 cattle and another only three; and again, one family has two sheep and another 101. The people tell me that the rats now eat about half the potato crop altogether, and of course are getting more numerous. I have been very busy every day since I came in serving out the provisions, etc., but everything is finished now, and by degrees I shall get my own things unpacked and arranged in my room. Today the family who live in the Church House, as they call it, are turning into a smaller house which has been unoccupied since the boat was lost. I used to have the house for a school when I was here before; but now I have got the loan of a large room in another house for the day-school, which will be much smaller and made up of much smaller children than formerly, as all my old boys have to go to work instead of their fathers, and I shall have them four nights a week *here* for night-school. Tomorrow the church will be properly arranged again, and we shall begin the regular routine of Sunday and weekday Services next week. Last Sunday we had matins and Evensong in the large room where Tom Glass used to have the Services before he was lost. I thought it better not to have any Celebration. I shall have a special Service of preparation on Saturday evening, and the first Celebration at 8 o'clock on Sunday. There are 39 of the old Communicants left, and four or five who, I think, are quite fit to be prepared for it. The Services last Sunday were very hearty and devout, with the same old chants as before, and hymns with more or less reference to the recent accident. I preached at Matins on the words out of the Gospel for the week, 'I have compassion on the multitude'. It was very hard to preach on that subject without breaking down, as so many of the people were in tears. I do feel so for the people. Of course they go on now much as usual, but some of the women look terribly broken down, and from time to time I can see that even the children have no means forgotten their loss. I have lived and eaten almost entirely in public since I came, for the people, old and young, seem to think that they can't look at me too much. I am sure it is their natural way of showing real affection for me, so I am quite content to let them do as they like. At this moment there are eight or nine children in the room. I got a draught-board and men at Madeira, and it has been in constant use ever since I unpacked it; but what all the young people are chiefly delighted with at present is that engine that runs of itself if you whirl round a heavy little wheel. The small children are delighted with the sweets and biscuits.

I believe now *all* the people wish to leave the island if it can only be arranged for them to have a fair start somewhere else. I have told them that it is my present intention not to leave them again until the looked-for opportunity arrives, for I feel that my work lies here to prepare the people for life in the world, and to teach the children. I see plainly that I shall be able to do much more personal work with the present young men than with the former generation of them, for they have all been schoolboys under me, and so are much more get-at-able, particularly now they have been so strangely forced into manhood by the loss of their fathers. I feel pretty confident that they will make excellent colonists when they get the chance, so I shall spare no pains with them at this most important era of their lives.

*Another cottage on the island*

Naturally, just at present, the roughness of the life here is not very palatable, but I shall soon get used to it again. One great help to me against discontent is a real warm affection for my people, and sympathy with them in their trouble, and also the feeling that my coming to be with them again really does cheer them up and please them in a way that no amount of letters could have done.

There is no fear of actual starving for some time to come, as the people say they have now in the huts enough potatoes to last till next January, when the new potatoes will be ready. All the women and elder girls have to work in the fields now as well as the boys. The two mongooses are being kept in their cages till the potato crop is pretty high, when they will be turned loose among them to carry on as much rat slaughter as they choose.

After a few days, Edwin wrote home again to his sisters, Fanny and Louisa. In this letter to Lizzie, dated 13 August 1886 (MS: Amy Irene Jaques Collection), he repeats some of the key points, which were clearly very much on his mind:

118

Dearest Lizzie,

Now for your turn. I tried to get Fanny's letter off this morning as the boat tried to catch a ship – but failed. I enclose a full statement of the statistics of the Island – the human contents of all the 15 houses, and the stock belonging to the inhabitants. I don't know of any other statistics which *can* be wanted. I never could get at the number of cattle and sheep before, for the people seemed to think that in some way or another that knowledge might be used to force them off the Island, but now that they all *want* to go, I had no difficulty whatever in getting the numbers! They all however stipulate for a 'fair offer' which will enable them to start a new life elsewhere, but as I find that no two people have the same ideas on that subject I think I have persuaded them to trust to *me* to decide on the fairness of the offer, so I think there will be no difficulty raised on *this* side of the water. I found that some of the people began to think that they didn't want to leave, now that *I* had come back, but I nipped that idea in the bud by assuring them all that if any offer of emigration was made to them which I considered reasonable, then, that whether *they* went or not, *I* should go, and not come back any more! And this declaration seems to have set the matter straight again. I begin the same old rounds of Service in the Church next Sunday and School work on Monday, and everything, I think, promises to go smoothly. As a set off against my determination to leave the Island, as soon as *they* all can, I have told them that it is my present intention not to leave them again until the looked-for opportunity arrives, for as starvation is *not* imminent, I feel that my work lies here to prepare the people for life in the world and to teach the children. Naturally just at present the roughness of the life here is not very palatable, but I shall soon get used to it again, and be able with a good heart to face another spell of isolation. All the way out from England I kept bothering myself with the pros and cons of 'to stay or not to stay' but when it came to the point of deciding I didn't feel the least shadow of a doubt as to my duty, nor have any doubts returned to bother me since. I feel sure that this *would* be the case when it came to the point, as my path of duty has always been made clear to me when the choice was actually before me. I see plainly that I shall be able to do much more real personal work with the present young men than I was able to do with the former generation of them – for this lot have all been schoolboys under me, and so are much more get-at-able, particularly now that they have been so strangely forced into manhood by the loss of their fathers. I feel pretty confident that they will make excellent Colonists when they get the chance, so I shall spare no pains with them at this the most important era of their lives. I wonder if that Queensland planter – I forget his name – would take the whole lot of people over there with their cattle, except the really old ones, who wish to go to their relations at the Cape, which will be decidedly the best place for them. I can't help hoping that this present year will see the wind up of this little settlement – it would be a marvellous relief to me! And then I could go and join the Bishop of Zululand in his work, which I should like *very* much, as I have such a special affection for Africans ... Captain Bosanquet gave me a revolver and cartridges for my protection, but I hope I shall never have to use it for *that* purpose. At present I find it very useful to lend to the young men to shoot their cattle with.

15/8/86 I have just come back from Mattins and have about two hours before me before taking the five Baptisms. I was busy all day yesterday in putting the Church in order for the beginning of Services today so I had no time for writing. We had the first Celebration at 8 a.m. Many of the Communicants did not receive today, which I am not at all surprised at, for I have no doubt they felt that after so long an interval they ought to take a little time to prepare themselves. They have certainly learnt *one* lesson here and that is an extreme reverence for Holy Communion – of course there was a full Congregation at Mattins, which was a very hearty Congregational Service as it always used to be. The singing and chanting sounds to me decidedly less harsh than formerly – perhaps a little nervousness on the part of the congregation may have made them rather subdue their voices. We had a lot of singing in my room the other night and I am delighted to find that my big treble boys have developed into good tenors and basses – or rather they *will* I hope, be good ones after a little training. The Services today seem so much more natural than they did last Sunday, now that we have got back into the old 'Church House' again. After the Celebration this morning an overwhelming feeling of responsibility and loneliness came over me at having to set all Parish machinery going again, but I hope in a week or two when I have got the daily routine of Church and School into *working* order, I shall feel much more reconciled to

Tristan life. One great help to me against irritation and discontent is a real warm affection for my people, and sympathy with them in their trouble, and also the feeling that my coming to be with them again really does please them and cheer them up in a way that no amount of letters could have done. I hope it is not presumption in me to find encouragement in what St. James says about 'Pure religion'. I always shrink from a *personal* application of texts containing encouragement or promises of reward for particular actions and habits, for all such things are sure to be so terribly marred by mixed motives. It must be very seldom that a good action is ever done with a perfectly pure motive. I'm sure none of *mine* ever are. It is wonderfully warm weather here for this time of year and the sea has been as calm as a duck pond every day since I came except last Sunday. I wish Captain Bosanquet had not been in such a fidget and got away for it would have been much more satisfactory if I had had time to send off these letters in the *Thalia* and there are a good many things which I could easily have got out of the ship which I now find I should much like to have for myself and also for the Islanders. I find that there is another plague on the Island besides the rats, and that is some kind of small insect which has destroyed *all* the tussocks which is used to thatch the houses with. If the roofs begin to leak now and are damaged by a gale of wind there is absolutely *nothing* to mend them with! They tell me that they believe that these insects came out of the same schooner that the rats did, but they never knew what they were 'up to' till last year. This is really a more serious plague than the rats for some of the roofs are in a very rotten condition and the people are at their wits end to know what to do with them. The Church roof is said to be one of the worst so I suppose we shall have rain dripping in upon us before long – a pleasing and helpful accompaniment to the Services! I am very much pleased to find what a completely different tone the people take about leaving the Island – they talk of it as a *reality* now – soon to be accomplished instead of a vague castle in the air which they didn't like the idea of. Oh I wish I was a rich man, and then I would then settle the whole business at once, for it really is now only a matter of £. s. d. – about £500 down and another £200 or £300 for a few years to provide 10 a week for the old people who are past work would do the whole thing except provide a passage for them, and that the Government might reasonably be expected to do as they *are* British subjects, for the Captain of one of the Men of War gave an English flag to the people to be hoisted on the Island, and if *that* does not imply that Tristan is an English Settlement I don't know what *would* do so! The Islanders are naturally most indignant at the notion of being repudiated by our Government, and even Captain Bosanquet declared that the Government might *say* what they liked, but that they *could* not really shirk their responsibility in the matter, and now that I hope the Conservatives are once more in Office, and in a strong *lasting* condition, I do most earnestly trust that they will find time to attend to this little lonely rock. I have just come back from Church and had my tea. I Baptized five children and Received one whom I had baptized privately just before I left Tristan. *Three* of the five were shortened! but only one cried and made itself straight and stiff, however by gripping it tight between my arm and side I managed not to drop it. I gave Loui's letter to go the round of the widows, and they have just told me that it is a very nice letter and very kind of her to write it, and they mean to answer it, but whether they will enclose the answer in one of my letters or send it separately I can't say. They were certainly very pleased to get it.

18/8/86 *Another* Man of War has just come here. I am going off to her directly to see who she is and what in the world she has come here for. I will enclose paper from the Islanders in my work. The people are all unanimous in declaring that the boat which was lost got quite close to the ship – certainly 400 yards, and she was seen to lower her sail as usual to go round the other side of the ship, which was then starting towards the boat, and the ship herself was so close to the Island that they could see a man standing looking over the stern – and the boat was never seen again, and they reckoned that in about 10 minutes after the boat would have been alongside, the ship squared away on her course. You see the story is completely contradictory to the Captain's own account. I can't make head nor tail of the matter. I am quite sure the people are saying what they believe to be true for I have cross examined them again and again about it. Best love,

Your very affectionate brother,
Edwin H. Dodgson

PS. This is some of the Rio paper money – 200 mil reis worth about 9½. Give it to Stuart.

Edwin's sisters sent gifts to the islanders. One of the islanders wrote this moving letter back to Edwin's sister Louisa thanking her, no doubt for her condolences in their tragic loss, and expressing her gratitude for having Edwin back to help and guide them. She was obviously one of the widows caused by the boating accident. The letter (MS: Amy Irene Jaques Collection) is dated 17 August 1886, and a few minor corrections have been made to the text.

Dear Friend,

In answer to your kind letter that we received from you we are happy to inform you that your dear Brother has returned safe and well back again to the island and as we did all we could to make him comfortable whilst he was with us before, we sincerely hope and trust by God's help we may be able so to do as long as it shall please God to let him remain with us. He has been very kind and good to us and did all he could to make us happy whilst he was with us and it is quite certain that he has thought and done everything he could for us when far away from us. And should it please God to remove him from us again we shall always esteem him as our best friend, teacher, minister and comforter as long as we live. Dear Friend you expressed your thanks to us for our kindness towards your dear Brother, we humbly accept them but consider our kindness very small in comparison for all that he has done for us. And dear friend as you have always prayed to our Heavenly Father to comfort and bless us, may you continue to ask Him to make us able to bear our great trouble and grief believing that all that has happened is His will and His will be done. And may you also pray to God for your dear Brother that he may enjoy good health and rest content that we will do all we can to make him happy. Dear friend we are not at all satisfied with the statement that the Captain gave about our lost boat, Husbands and friends. His statement is quite a mystery to us and should your dear Brother succeed in a fair arrangement for us we, with him, may better ourselves in some other land. We were very thankful for the help and provisions that your dear Brother interceded for and brought us – it was a very present help now in the time of need. And now dear friend we express our greatest and sincere thanks for the dresses you so kindly sent each of us widows and as you have given unto us, may God in His great Mercy give unto you dear friend. You said you know that we would be glad to see your dear Brother again, we were truly glad to see him for believe us dear friend in our deepest sorrow he brought us joy. And now my dearest friend we conclude and may the blessing of God be with you is the heartfelt wish of the Widows and the community of Tristan d'Acunha to their dear friend, Miss Louisa Dodgson.

Captain Bosanquet of HMS *Thalia* reported the condition of the inhabitants of Tristan da Cunha to the Admiralty, his report reaching them in September 1886. He said that the distress that they were supposed to be suffering was not as bad as had been suggested, but bad enough to give some concerns about their future. The potato crop had not been destroyed by the rats; a hundred bushels had been sold to passing ships during the past year, and they had enough in hand to last until the next season, together with six hundred bushels of seed potatoes. There were five hundred cattle on the island, but some had been washed away in a recent flood. Each family had one or two cows giving milk.

During the past year only two whalers and eight other ships had visited the island, all small craft that did not carry surplus stores. As a result, the islanders had only been able to trade one sheep and a hundred bushels of potatoes for a small quantity of flour, a few pounds of tea and sugar, and a very small quantity of clothing.

The rats were becoming very numerous, and defied the efforts of the islanders to destroy them. If they continued to multiply at the same rate, it was feared that in a year or two the potato crop would fail, thus making it difficult for the islanders to survive.

Captain Bosanquet's report continued:

These people are not anxious about their condition, because they are confident that the English Government is bound to support them. To all argument they return the simple answer, 'We live under the English law.'

It is evident that the cattle could not be removed, and that the people could not be sent away absolutely penniless. It seems advisable, therefore, to consider their case with a view to their eventual removal (should the potato crop fail), and to propose terms of compensation to them, which would altogether clear the island, and enable the people to become self-supporting members of some more flourishing community.

Should the removal of the inhabitants be contemplated, it seem likely that a free passage and £5 a head would clear the island, except in the case of a few old men and women without families, who, being unable to work, could not be left if the younger people and those with families were removed. Separate terms should, therefore, be proposed to these aged persons, who in number amount to about eight, viz. three men and five women.

Considering the matter of cost to the public funds, it is evident that the expenditure of a sum of money in removing the islanders to a locality where they could become self-supporting would be more than covered by the saving in expenses of provisions, stores, and clothing, which will have to be frequently sent to the island if the people are to be kept from starving.

The older people would probably not take kindly to any change, but the younger people and children would be saved much privation and hardship in the future and become useful colonists in South Australia.

There can be no doubt that Captain Bosanquet's report was strongly influenced by Edwin's views concerning relocation.

On 18 August 1886, the captain of another passing ship, HMS *Rapid*, wrote a similar report, which indicated that 'Mr. Dodgson appeared, in the course of a few days, to have inspired the islanders with the idea that they would like to leave if given a £5 gratuity.' The report continued, 'He [Edwin Dodgson] stated that gratuitous supplies were unnecessary, as they tended to the loss of self-respect and fostered the laziness which was ascribed to the Tristanites.'

Probably unbeknown to Edwin, the Admiralty considered the various reports they had received over the previous months, and issued a proclamation which was sent to Rear-Admiral Sir Walter Hunt Grubbe, commander-in-chief of the Cape Station, dated 20 November 1886:

Sir,

Referring to your letter, forwarding a report of the proceedings of H.M.S. *Rapid* at Tristan d'Acunha, dated 28th August, I am commanded by my Lords Commissioners of the Admiralty to acquaint you that they concur with you as to the feasibility of an annual visit to one of Her Majesty's ships of war on the station under your command to the Island of Tristan d'Acunha.

My Lords accordingly desire that you will arrange for such a visit to be made annually, at suitable seasons, and when the other duties of the station will admit of it.

With reference to the question of the issue of stores to the islanders, adverted to in your submission above quoted, and in yours of the 31st August, my Lords have been in communication with Her Majesty's Treasury and the Secretary of State for the Colonies; and they desire to lay down as a general rule that no provisions or stores are to be issued to the inhabitants of Tristan d'Acunha from Her Majesty's ships visiting the island, except on repayment in money or in kind.

If, however, it should appear to the officer in command of the vessel visiting the island to be absolutely necessary to issue some supplies to alleviate unavoidable distress, due to the failure of crops, the loss of stock, or other disaster, for which supplies the inhabitants have really no means of repayment, he is to use his own discretion in making such issues as he may deem to be absolutely necessary, reporting fully the circumstances of the case, and furnishing a list of the stores supplied and their value.

The British government were clearly of the opinion that the settlement on Tristan should remain, in order that passing ships, including those of Her Majesty's Navy, should be able to restock with food and water, and the island remain a lifeline to ships wrecked in the treacherous waters of the South Atlantic. For their part, they were willing to support the islanders, but not to undermine their ability to be self-sufficient and hard-working. Supplies were to be issued with discretion and only in extreme circumstances.

Edwin remained on the island for another three years. Meanwhile, life continued as before on Tristan, as Edwin reported in a letter to his sister Margaret. The letter, dated 3 December 1886, is now incomplete (MS: Amy Irene Jaques Collection):

Dearest Maggie,

It is rather strange that it should happen to come to *your* turn to have my Christmas budget, so I will begin by wishing you many happy returns of your birthday, though that day will probably be long past before you get my wishes, if you ever *do* get them, but that can't be helped. We have had no Whaler from St. Helena yet, so I wait in vain for any 'good news from home'. Patience is a great virtue and if you wish to acquire it you cannot do better than come and live at Tristan for a few years. I am just convalescent from the longest and most overpowering bout of headache I have had since I came here. I completely collapsed after morning school last Monday and did nothing else all the rest of the week except Celebrate on Thursday morning, which I *just* managed to get through without breaking down. I could get very little sleep at night, so on Saturday night I rather reluctantly took an opiate in the shape of 15 drops of tincture of opium and that gave me some hours of sound sleep so that I got through the Service yesterday all right and I have School and Church today as usual without any bad effects, though my head is still very weak. Old Mrs. Cotton caught a bad cold about a fortnight ago and has been getting weaker and weaker ever since, and for the last week she has been entirely laid up, and as I believe she is about 80 years old I have little doubt that her end is coming very near – she thinks so herself. Being in the same house with her I can visit her constantly, and as far as I can judge she is quite prepared for her call. She has never learnt to read, but she is a very good old woman and has been a most regular Communicant. I gave her the H.C. this morning and 17 of the people came and Communicated with her, chiefly her own children and grandchildren. She has four daughters and two sons married on the Island besides one unmarried daughter who lives with her, and another daughter a widow without children, and 28 grandchildren and 2 great grandchildren on the Island. Mrs. Cotton is the oldest inhabitant here both as to her own age and in the number of years she has been on the Island. She is the last survivor of the 5 St. Helena women who came here on spec to marry the 5 men who were the only people here except Glass and his wife and children about 40 years ago. Mrs. Cotton seems decidedly to have got the best husband, and in spite of the hap hazard way they began their married life, they got to be a very loving couple and really seem to have done their best to bring up their children religiously – my little godson Arthur Edwin Green is one of her grandchildren, for three of her [incomplete]

Back in England, Charles continued his efforts to secure resettlement for the islanders. He wrote again to Lord Salisbury on 21 February 1887 (MS: Hatfield). Lord Salisbury was now in his second term as Prime Minister and Foreign Secretary.

Dear Lord Salisbury,
    May I take up a few minutes of your time with the matter of Tristan d'Acunha, and the transmigration of its people, about which you kindly gave me and my brother (the Rev. E. H. Dodgson, who has been 'priest in charge' there for 4 years) an interview a year ago.
    The Admiralty gave my brother a free passage, to return there last March, and also sent out some stores (such as potatoes) as the people were in much need, owing to a plague of rats, who devoured their crops. My brother had come to England (as you may remember) to try to manage the transference of the people to some other quarter (Australia, probably), as there is no reason now for any one living there at all: whalers used to visit it, but, now that the whales come no more, no one goes near it. 15 of the men were lost at sea lately, and there are now only 11 able-bodied men, and only about 90 altogether, counting women and children. To transfer the *people* only would be a very small matter, but it would be most desirable, if possible, to take their cattle and sheep to the Cape, where, if they can be got there alive, they would sell for about £10,000, and thus furnish means for starting the people in life elsewhere.

I am informed that the captain of the *Thalia* (which took my brother there), was told to report on the subject of the Government undertaking the removal of the people (who are anxious to go) and that he has reported to the Admiralty in favour of its being done.

What I chiefly write about now is to say that I have received from my brother two papers – one a list of the people, with ages and amount of cattle, etc. – the other a statement, signed by the heads of families, of their willingness to leave the island. I do not know what I ought to do with these papers. Should I write to the Admiralty about them?

My brother is *most* anxious to get these poor people moved into the world, and to be free himself for mission-work in Africa. He is being simply *wasted* at present, in looking after these few dozen people, and living as a second Robinson Crusoe.

Sincerely yours,

C. L. Dodgson

The tone of the letter is one of desperation. It was unlikely to elicit any response because the government had already made their decision about the fate of the islanders, as reported to the commander-in-chief of the Cape (see above). Lord Salisbury was fully aware of the government's position. However, he did offer an alternative option. In a letter dated 24 February 1887 (MS copy: Hatfield), Lord Salisbury suggested that some ship owner at the Cape be invited to undertake the operation, using the value of the cattle as a means of financing the venture. Charles renewed his acquaintance with George Baden Powell, who had tried to help previously, in the hopes of getting his guidance, and wrote in his diary on 29 March 1887:

Went to town for day. Called on Mr. Baden Powell, and had a talk about Tristan. He suggested that perhaps some one might be found at the Cape, who would buy the cattle where they are, and remove them at his own expense.

Also he agreed that I had better write to urge Edwin to get the people to agree to a fairly equal division of proceeds of sale.

He advised me to see a 'Mr. Arnold White', who is an enthusiast in emigration, and promised to write to him about me.

Arnold White (1848–1925) was a journalist living at Brunswick Place, London, with his wife, Helen Constance née Price (1849–1918), and son, Lowell (b. 1879). He wrote 'Common Sense of Colonial Emigration' for the *Contemporary Review* in March 1886, and stood unsuccessfully as a Liberal MP for Mile End later in the year. However, Charles did not appear to make contact with him.

A few months later, Charles was again seeking support from Lord Salisbury, preparing the ground by writing to Lord Salisbury's daughter Gwendolen (1860–1945). He recorded on 14 May 1887:

> To town for the day, with Maggie Earle as my companion ... Then to Lord Salisbury's, as I wanted to ask about the chance of getting introduced to some ship-owner (about which I had written to Gwendolen), and to ask Lord Salisbury if the Government would consent to the island of Tristan being depopulated. He was not in: but we saw Lady Salisbury, Maud, and Gwendolen.

Edwin continued to send reports back to his sisters of how life was for the islanders, and how he himself was coping. This letter to Louisa is dated 14 April 1887 (MS: Amy Irene Jaques Collection):

> Dearest Loui,
>     Mary's budget took to itself wings yesterday, so I will go ahead at yours to make a start at all events. I had a little practice in signalling and reading signals yesterday, as a ship came within reach and hoisted her colours, which for a long time we could not distinguish as she was so far off, but after several erroneous guesses, I at length got a clear sight of them as Norwegian – rather a disappointment, as by the red ground I really thought that at last we were going to have an *English* ship – The English merchantmen's flag is what is called the 'red ensign' – red with blue union Jack in the corner – the Norwegian flag is red with a blue straight cross full length and width with a narrow white edge to it. I asked him 'what's o'clock?' – he immediately in reply told me his name, or rather *meant* to do so, but it afterwards appeared from a note he sent over that he had hoisted one of the four flags wrong – 'S' for 'F' – very stupid of him – but

probably he called out 'F' to the signal man, who thought he said 'S'.

15/4/87 I have begun my school work again today. It is very dreary work … but it is an excellent school for learning patience and perseverance for the *master*, so in fact the children are the *teachers*, and I am the *learner*, or rather I *ought* to be. I often think about poor Clara Wilcox[44] – her life in this world must seem very dark and lonely, but as Miss Yonge says in one of her books 'time *does* somehow fill up the holes in one's life by degrees' and, after all, her grief – bitter as it must be – is only, I am thankful to think, for *herself*, and not for her husband. I can't help feeling, as I tell my people, that in brooding over such *personal* grief there is a serious danger of our feeling *really* becoming *murmuring against God* in our hearts, however much we might disclaim such an idea with our *lips*. I suppose if our faith and unselfishness were *perfect* the intense joy of feeling that one we loved was in perfect peace and safety for ever would entirely swallow up our personal sense of temporary loss. The hymn 'Christ will gather in his own' is very beautiful, but surely as to the very beginning 'Had Christ asked us etc.', though no doubt it *is* a perfectly true picture of the feeling of most of us, yet it *ought* not to be so, and I think we shall be ashamed to have given way to such feelings when we are once more living with our dear ones in Paradise, if by God's mercy we are permitted to enter there. I daresay these ideas may seem to you to be very high flown and visionary, but I think there must be something in them as I always feel them most strongly when I can most clearly realize 'beyond the grave'. Do you know that rather striking little book 'The Gate's ajar'? It is a good many years since I read it, but I think it is founded on the same line of thought.[45] I gave my usual short address at Mattins this morning on Thessalonians IV.14. that if we *really and truly* believed in the other world as much as in this world we should grieve far less at any one we loved having 'departed in peace', than if they had gone away to some other part of *this* world, where they might be exposed to all manner of temptations, and might fall away from God. I have a sort

---

[44] In 1886, Edwin's cousin Clara Wilcox lost her husband, William Lane Hitchcock, twenty-six, after being married for just three years.

[45] *The Gate's Ajar* was a sentimental and didactic novel by Elizabeth Stuart Phelps Ward about a girl's struggle to renew her faith after the death of a beloved brother.

of vague hope that you have tried the same plan of sending off printed copies of a letter here as I did, so that I feel that it is *just* possible that any passing ship may bring me a copy. I mean of course any *English* ship, but these seem now to be extinct. A file of English newspapers would be an *unspeakable* treat, and it would be an intense relief to be assured of one single fact, i.e. that my letters of last October had been received and their 'contents duly noted' – to use a commercial phrase. I wonder what Captain Bosanquet reported to the Admiralty about Tristan! His last words to me were 'I don't think you will be left very long on the Island' but whether he had any practical intentions on the subject or whether these words were only a vague kind wish *I* cannot say, but *you* will have known long before this.

18/4/87 The wind has been in the South since yesterday, and this afternoon it has gone round to North-East and I think it will be due North in a few hours. This course of proceeding has a very 'shippy' look about it. The South wind keeps vessels back, so as to 'pile them up' so to speak. The North-East wind brings them down into our latitudes to the West of the Island so that they generally come across the Island pretty handy with a North wind – but tomorrow will shew. If *English* ships still go on *not* coming I think something ought to be done about it, for we can't make out where in the world all the English ships can have got to. I spent about an hour the other day in a way quite unprecedented during my sojourning here – in reading – or rather re-reading – that well-known sensational novel 'Called Back'. It had been given to one of the boys by someone on board the last ship which they boarded, I think – it was rather a treat. The boys often get old books given them by passing ships, which are generally handed on to me and in most cases turn out to be most utter rubbish. I believe this is really the *first* time that any book worth reading has found its way here in this manner.

22/4/87 A ship is slowly coming this way from the Westward as I will try and get this letter off by her, if you will not mind my writing it with the help of an infidel's 'pince-nez' – my eyes have been very painful for the last few days. Last night I gave up reading as a bad job and dozed instead in my armchair from about 7.30 to 9.30 when we had prayers. I don't know what is the matter with the said eyes, but I hope the evil is only a temporary one. They don't burn much by daylight. If I read with blue glasses – but by candlelight they get very 'contrary' and even in reading the Lesson in Church the air between me and the Bible is very cloudy and restless, so that I make a good many verbal mistakes. I can't *see* anything the matter with my eyes in the looking glass, and it is not quite convenient to consult an oculist at present! I wish I had a pair of blue goggles instead of these 'pince nez' – they are so much more comfortable, but alas the pair which I used to use sometimes in Zanzibar has been lying at the bottom of the sea off the rocks here for nearly six years. We had rather a fright here on Wednesday. Some of the boys were trying to split a huge log with blasting powder and some how or another one of the blasts went off within 2 feet of one of them. Luckily most of the force was expended upon the wood, but it burnt his face very much and I fear very deeply, as it bled so much. Now his face and eyes are all swollen up and as black as a coal, but I don't *think* his sight is destroyed, for he was able to see certainly with *one* of his eyes, before it swelled up. He is using the last remains of that jar of linseed oil and lime water, which I brought with me when I first came, and which washed up unbroken. I'm afraid there are a good many bits of blasting powder left in his face, for the grains are bigger than peas, and his face was much torn, but I hope they will work out of themselves as *I* don't know how to deal with them. He feels very little pain which I'm afraid is not a very good sign, but he is in God's hands. He is a regular Communicant and I have always thought him a remarkably good boy as far as I can judge. He is about 16 or 17 years old. This would be a glorious day for general embarkation, as the sea is a dead level and there is only just enough wind to keep the air fresh, but it is too soon yet for any such 'lump of delight'. I tell the people that such a thing *may* come to pass about July.

Now I must stop. Best love,

Your very affectionate brother,

E. H. Dodgson

23/4/87 That ship to the westward never came within reach after all, but this afternoon a few of the boys went off to try to catch a ship a long way off – rather a wild goose chase – but if it hadn't come on very rainy and foggy I believe they would have caught her – as it is they just brought this letter ashore again so it must wait a little longer. The burnt boy's face seems to be getting on very well. The right side, the least hurt of the two, is beginning to resume its natural colour more or less and he can see a little out of the right eye. *My* eyes are *much* better tonight and I am writing this bit by candlelight without glasses without discomfort, so I hope they won't bother me any longer. Good bye.

The government continued to get reports from the island, prepared by the captains of Her Majesty's ships making their annual visit. Commander W E B Atkinson[46] of HMS *Acorn* sent a report dated February 1888. On this occasion, one family of nine persons (mother, three sons, four daughters and one granddaughter) requested transport to the Cape. This was granted. The ship's surgeon, Dr Maitland, vaccinated a number of children.

Commander Atkinson wrote about the condition of the islanders, stating that 'there is no poverty of any kind on Tristan; the people are mostly dressed in a sort of dungaree which they obtain from the American whalers.' He indicated that the islanders preferred money to stores in their trading deals, probably because 'the impression left on my mind, whether right or wrong, is that these people intend leaving the island and emigrating to America and Australia.'

On 14 April 1888, Charles published a letter in the *St James's Gazette* seeking personal support for his brother. The letter, addressed to the editor, appeared on 16 April under the heading 'Tristan d'Acunha':

---

[46] William Edward Breeks Atkinson (b. 1846) was captain of HMS *Acorn* from 1887 until 1889, when he retired from the Royal Navy.

Sir,

Will you kindly grant me space, in your columns, to ask if any clergyman, who takes in the *Guardian*, would bestow his copy, when done with, on my brother, the Rev. E. H. Dodgson, who is 'Priest in Charge' in the lonely island of Tristan d'Acunha, 1,200 miles from the nearest land – S. Helena. Communications between S. Helena and Tristan are 'few and far between', and my brother lives almost as if in another planet, so little does he hear of what goes on in the busy world he has left in order to devote himself to the spiritual needs of these poor islanders. When any vessel does go, it of course takes whatever letters etc. have accumulated for him at S. Helena and a batch of old *Guardians* would be very welcome to him, even if months old when they reach him.

If any brother-priest will do him this service, I shall be grateful for a line, addressed to me at Oxford, that I may arrange with him as to where, and when, the papers should be sent. – I am, Sir,

Your obedient servant,

Charles L. Dodgson

Christ Church, Oxford

Edwin continued to encourage some of the islanders to leave Tristan and begin a new life elsewhere. This extract from a letter dated June 1888 gives some indication of his success in this matter (MS: Amy Irene Jaques Collection):

I have heard from Captain Bruno, the Commissariat Officer at St. Helena. He tells me that the boat was to cost about £35 and that he expected it at St. Helena from the States last April and he would forward it here by the next Man-of-War. He offers to do anything for me, but unfortunately things at St. Helena are just double the price they are in England. The S.P.G. 'honorarium' came in very handy and has already enabled me to help 8 people to leave the Island in the *Curaçoa*, and I hope 12 men will be able to get away in the *next* Man-of-War. Of course exporting the people by *retail* can only be done for a limited time as it would never do for *all* the workers to leave the non-workers here alone to shift for themselves, but *at present* it is all right. As to the eye stones, how do you account for them moving about under a person's eyelid and 'cleaning' the eye, which I am assured they do? Your carbonic-acid-gas theory *may* be true as regards the *vinegar*, but if you watch them closely as they move you will see that they have a lot of fine hair-like legs which come out of the shell or stone or whatever it is. So I think there *must* be some kind of *animal* life in them.[47] If ever I come back to England I will try to bring a lot more with me, as there are plenty here. The American Whalers use them largely and introduced them here, and Captain Hagan has used them *himself* for 'eye cleaning' – so their capability in this way is not merely legendary. I have been much interested in the Διδαχη – many thanks for it and also for the other books all of which are most enjoyable. I object strongly to *Knight Errant* being called a 'novel' – it is a most striking Sermon – on 'If any man will come after ME etc.' only Carlo is too good for a human being. Whether the course he took was *actually* the *best* is, I think, very doubtful, but he certainly acted on the purest motives, but why did he *go on* as an opera singer after Nita's death? Bishop Shere's life is of course of most thrilling interest to me and also Mr. Macan's books about Kuingani (or Kuinua Mguu as it is more properly called). As to reading stories to the people it would be utterly useless. In the first place because 'book-English' is like a foreign language to them and also no stories could possibly interest them as they know nothing of anything beyond Tristan. Please thank Mr. Slatter and Canon Argles for the £6. I suppose the clothes, boots, etc. were the produce of their kindness. I don't think I know either of them *personally*. Best love to all

Your very affectionate brother,

E. H. Dodgson

---

[47] Edwin's reference to eye stones is interesting. He correctly identifies their eye cleansing function; one medical dictionary defines eye stones as 'very small stones placed in the conjunctival sac to remove a mobile foreign body from the eye'. Visitors to Holbox – an unspoilt island off Mexico – have described eye stones as shell eyes used for the same purpose. A third definition suggests that an eye stone is a 'small smooth shell or other object that is inserted between the eyelid and the eye for the purpose of removing foreign substances from the eye'. Edwin's reference to 'hair-like legs' is more puzzling given that references to the stones do not suggest that they are animate.

Another visit was made to Tristan by HMS *Curaçoa* in December 1888. Captain R A Stopford brought with him a whale boat which he sold to the islanders; they were very grateful to obtain it. The islanders also received supplies and clothing to the value of £45, for which they traded a small quantity of potatoes – all they could spare since their current crop had been seriously affected by blight. Captain Stopford also gave some medicines, a rifle, some ammunition and a small fishing boat to the islanders. He reported his system for dealing with the islanders, giving advice to other captains calling at Tristan. He explained that Edwin ascertained the islanders' wants from a list of provisions and clothing that could be spared, with prices marked against them, and calculated what could be given in exchange. Captain Stopford's opinion was that:

> ... the pastor was the only one on the island capable of ascertaining the islanders' wants, and in case of his absence this would have to be done by an officer from the ship. This need not be a lengthy process, as the unwritten law of the island required all trading to be done by the heads of families.

Edwin Dodgson was the only person on the island who could make a signal using the Mercantile Code, and passing ships would call less frequently if Edwin were not there.

In 1888, only five ships had called at Tristan, and the lack of trade had become so serious that often the only food to eat was meat and potatoes. Edwin reported that he had had no bread for over two months, and no tea for ten months.

Edwin shared his concerns with his brother Charles in a letter dated 20 December 1888 (MS: Amy Irene Jaques Collection):

> Dear Charles,
>     As your letters want a good deal of answering, I think I had better begin on them at once. First a few general remarks and then I will go through them in detail. I wish I could make you understand once for all (a) that the people here are *not starving – bodily* nor are they in any present danger of it (b) as my reasons for wishing so earnestly to

remove them are extremely spiritual and not *temporal*, I *know* perfectly well that the Government cannot be expected to take any steps about it. The late distress was a mere temporary accident arising from the loss of the life-boat. Now that the boys are rapidly becoming men, they can more and more take their fathers' places and do the necessary field work, and strange to say, the rats though largely on the increase, are doing less harm to the potato crop than they did at first! So that as regards *temporalia* the Islands are no worse off, or not much worse off than they were 8 years ago.

I am getting to see more and more plainly that it would be utterly unreasonable in me to expect any one to take my view of the case. No one can possibly know what the Tristanites *really are* without living here, and I have no doubt that what I say and write about their non-intellectuality (to coin a new word) seem mere ... exaggerations. This I feel is only natural and indeed *inevitable* so that I can do nothing more in the matter except by prayer – unless God should ever place enough means at my disposal to carry out my wishes.

I wish you could ascertain from the agent of the *Queensland* Government (his office is somewhere in Victoria Street I think) what it would cost (of course, roughly speaking) to settle the people in that colony. If the population here consisted only of young men and boys, I was told by a Queensland planter that the Government would gladly send one of their own ships for them at their own expense – but the women and children and old people are a difficulty this man told me. The colony was 'too young' to maintain any other than *workers* – but this was nearly 4 years ago, so they may have changed their minds now. If the Queensland Government chose to undertake to provide for the whole lot of people for the sake of getting the workers, and would send for them, the matter could be at once arranged without difficulty, and the relief to my mind would be beyond the power of words to describe – the 'good effected by the terriers and mongooses' is *nil*!

I should say that Captain Atkinson's 'Report of the Island' is not worth the paper it is written on, judging by your quotations! I should be curious to know whether he mentions sending back a boat-load of geese etc. which were taken to the 'Acorn' with a list of stores wanted in exchange *in accordance with his request*, and what *reason* he gives for so doing – geese etc. are the only *money* the people have.

I presume Capt. Atkinson paid Mrs. Beetham (the passenger) for the sheep and potatoes he *did* take – if not, all I can say is he got them remarkably cheap, as he gave *us* nothing for them! ...

Now as to your most kind offer of sending out a locum tenens from time to time ... I will try and make you understand what I think about it. In the first place I do *not* think that such a treat is *necessary for my health* and as I do not feel that such a change is *necessary* I cannot make up my mind whether I should be justified in accepting so much money to spend upon my *pleasure* – but then again, I am bothered with the idea that a visit to England would not be only a *selfish* pleasure.

I don't think I have ever been in such a quandary before. I simply *cannot* decide one way or the other. I really do want to do what is right in the matter, so I will leave it to you to decide. If on consideration you send out a locum tenens here, I will come home, but if you decide *not* to send any one, I shall be quite content to stay on here as long as God pleases. If I could take a short holiday, for a couple of months or so, then I should have no hesitation in doing so – but to come away for at least a year, and perhaps considerably longer, almost seems like 'looking back'. You see how I am swayed about, so please decide as you think best. I put myself in your hands – whichever way you decide I shall be equally grateful to you for the *offer*. In fact you can understand that the mere fact of *having had* such an offer will of itself be a refreshment. I suppose there always *must* be more or less difficulty in decisions according to the amount of *pleasure* involved. In this case there is so *much* pleasure involved that I *dare not* trust my own judgement, and as God has not made the matter clear to me one way or the other, I don't think He can mean *me* to decide it. I think that if I were alone in the world I should see my way quite clearly to decide an offer to spend so much money on my *personal* pleasure, but situated as I am I can only leave the matter in your hands.

Do you really think that I ought to change for some *paying* work? My own feeling about it is that as God so plainly sent me here, it is safer to put myself altogether into *His* Hands for direction as to my sphere of work.

The Proprietors of the 'Guardian' are 'bricks', and I shall tell them so, though perhaps 'not in those precise words'! I think I have now commented on your letter as much, and probably more, than you can desire. I really am ashamed of the enormous length of the letter, and tremble to think of the postage that *somebody* will have to pay.

I don't know whether my letter to the Admiralty was the *cause*, but certainly Capt. Stopford of the *Curaçoa* acted in his trading with us *exactly* as I could have wished and in direct contrast to the wretched '*Acorn*' man. One of the first things he said to me was 'I *want nothing*, but I have come here "for your good"' (meaning of course the good of the Islanders). He brought a price list of the stores he could supply, and was ready to take Island produce in exchange in any quantities, except *live* bullocks and pigs. I arranged with him what value he would give for the different things, and he returned on board, leaving the Doctor on shore to vaccinate etc. I then had very plain sailing work to do. I had each head-of-a-family come to me one by one. They first told me what they wanted to sell, and then having told what value Capt. Stopford would give them for the things, they each chose from his list of stores just the things and quantities they wished for up to that amount. My work was quite simple, only involving a succession of short practice sums, so I soon had two lists – one of the stock, etc. the people were sending off to the ship, and the other, the stores, quantity and quality wanted in exchange. These two lists I took off to the ship (as the Capt. had asked me to lunch with him), and the Paymaster issued the amount of the different stores, and checked off the produce sent, by my list. The whole business went like a newly cleaned clock, and *nobody grumbled*! Indeed there was nothing which anybody *could* grumble at. I literally worried a present of a small fishing boat out of Capt. Stopford. He suggested I should pay £28 for it – I declined the proposal without the *slightest hesitation*, and so got the boat and fittings gratis. He made me sign 6 receipts for it, but I considered even *that* preferable to paying £28!

Many thanks for all the trouble you have taken about the new whale boat. Capt. Bruno writes me word that it will be at St. Helena next April – and I am writing to the Admiralty – and also to the Admiral at the Cape – imploring that a man-of-war may be sent from the Cape to bring it to us before the winter. I shall be much surprised if they grant my request, but 'nothing venture, nothing *get*'. I have suggested to the people that they should bring the money for it to *me* as soon as possible, so that I may be able to hand it over in a lump to the Capt. of the man-of-war which brings it here. I like to have things ready *beforehand*. The Doctor was absurdly careful about the medicine he sent people – he not only labelled each bottle with the fullest directions, but gave me besides an elaborately drawn up *paper* of directions, and also reiterated the directions to me *vivâvoce, usque ad nauseam*. I should like to know whether the doctor of the '*Acorn*' 'caught it' from the Admiralty for his gross carelessness in sending a bottle without any label on it, which I complained of in my letter. I *hope* he did. Captain Stopford sent his own boat on shore for me, and hauled me on board in an armchair, as I told him that I *couldn't* climb up the side of the ship. He supplied me with a box of candles – 50 lbs. I had proposed to *buy* 20 lbs, but I was quite willing to adopt his amendment, and he returned the compliment by adopting *mine* in regard to the fishing boat. I wish all Naval Captains were like him. He is out and out the best that has ever been here. He also gave me a Martini Henry rifle, and 200 cartridges to shoot cattle with. In fact I believe he would have given me *anything*! In my letter to the Admiralty I expressed much gratitude to him for his 'kindness and consideration'. I wanted their Lordships to see that I could appreciate a brick as well as blame an idiot – and a little 'butter' may soften their hearts with regard to our whale boat.

Ever your affectionate and grateful brother,

E. H. Dodgson

In an incomplete letter (the rest is missing), Edwin reports the discomfort caused by the poor weather, the lack of food, and his uphill task of providing spiritual guidance to the islanders. The deterioration in his health and the resultant onset of depression are clearly evident in this letter to Louisa, dated 27 June 1889 (MS: Amy Irene Jaques Collection):

Many thanks for your six letters and also for the Altar linen – comforters, etc. I have just succeeded, I hope, in stopping the rain coming on the Altar – it comes in freely in other parts of the Church.

The thatched roof is quite rotten, but unfortunately there is no tussock now to renew it with – it has all been killed presumably by some insect. If any of the house roofs are blown away this winter I don't know *what* the unfortunate inmates can do! We haven't had any *regular* gale yet – only half a gale, but I was twice blown down a few Sundays ago on my way to the early Celebration in the dark – or rather moonlight – and the other morning I fell into a hole about 2 feet deep, which had been scooped out by the heavy rain during the night. So you see *I* tumble about nearly as much as *you* do! Ships seem to have given up coming near here – we have only had two Merchantmen and *no* Whalers since the 11th of last October, and we have long been out of all imports. This morning I breakfasted on arrowroot flavoured with macaroni! which I got from the *Curaçoa*. I have been very unwell for the last two days and have not been out of doors at all – I think I may now say for certain that a potato diet does *not* suit me, but I would gladly never taste flour again if I could feel that I was doing the people any good. *No* one – old or young – seem to take the slightest *interest* in religion. I suppose it is the natural consequence of their minds being incapable of understanding more than mere *surface* Religion, but it is very dreary work for me trying to make chairs and tables without any wood! I am getting to feel more and more irritable every day, but I am thankful to say that hitherto I have been able to suppress all outward signs of it. The only effect of freedom from many temptations is, as far as I can see, to make the Tristanites mere 'fair weather' Christians. I believe it would be *much* better for them to be brought up in the East End. I mean of course *humanly* speaking, for no doubt there are some good reasons for them being imprisoned here. *I* can see nothing but harm in their isolation ...

Writing to his brother Skeffington on 12 July 1889, Edwin described the current situation on the island (MS: Amy Irene Jaques Collection):

Dear Skeff,

Many thanks for your letter which I got last December by the *Curaçoa*. It certainly well deserves an answer and it shall have one, but if the answer will ever have a chance of getting to England is quite another matter. We have only been able to board two Merchant vessels since the 11th of last October and *no* Whalers. It has never happened here before that a whole summer has gone by without a single Whaler calling, but it has been so *last* summer. I suppose the Whales must have shifted their ground. I saw one 'spouting' about a mile off last September or August, but while I was in England a Whaler managed to catch a big one close to the beach here to the great delight of the Tristanites. I should have liked to have seen the hunt and capture. During my stay here before I came back to England I have seen them playing in the sea here rolling about like huge black sausages. You ask me about 'Yesterday, Today, and Forever'. I like this book very much on the whole. The first part about the death of the seer and his going to Paradise is *very* beautiful, and I have read it again and again. I didn't care much about the 'Millennium' for of course it is all imaginary, as we really *know nothing* about that mystery, and the 'Judgement' is, I think, too awful to represent, for we have no Divine Guide to the *details* of that Day. The real scene is no doubt so *far* beyond the grasp of human understanding that I should fear that any attempt to realize it might lead to sceptical questions as to 'How can these things be?' Trying to see more than is in sight is the basis of the infidel's rule 'quod non videndum, non credendum'. I was glad to hear that you had got into more comfortable quarters than you were in when I saw you at the Chestnuts. I hope your children are flourishing. I heard that you had lost two little boys. I suppose parents must feel the loss even of a young baby at the time, but I should think that such a feeling must be *very* temporary, and entirely swallowed up in the exceeding joy of having at all events *one* child safe for ever. The children here are wonderfully healthy. Any ailments are almost unknown, and the way they can eat unripe apples and raw cabbage stalks makes me shudder. You probably know that Charles has most kindly offered to send a *locum tenens* here for a year, so as to give me a little change, but I don't know whether he will carry out this idea or not – anyone who came here must be quite prepared to do without most things, which are generally thought necessaries, especially in the way of food, and of course he would have to 'rough it' to any extent. I have got so used to the life here now that of course I don't feel these sort of things nearly as much as a *new* comer would. I shall send this letter to Guildford, if ever I can send it anywhere away from here –

even if we do not get any more Merchantmen, I suppose there is pretty sure to be a Man-of-War calling here during the next six months, for I believe the Admiralty have arranged to send one here every year. If one *does* come here from St. Helena, I shall hope to get another file of *Guardian*s, from the Proprietors of the paper [who] post me a copy to St. Helena gratis every week. I have had no news since the 14th of November 1888, so that another batch of papers etc. will be very acceptable, and the Bishop of St. Helena always sends me his copies of the *Mail* (the condensed edition of the *Times* published 3 times a week). I remember Irene being at the Chestnuts when I was last at home, or rather to speak more accurately that *you* and Isa had a baby with you there, which I presume was Irene.[48] She must be growing quite a big girl by this time. I wonder which of her numerous relatives she takes after in appearance. I could never have come here if I had been a family man for it would be utterly out of the question for any lady to live at Tristan. Now with all good wishes for yourself, Isa, and your children, I remain

Your very affectionate brother,
Edwin H. Dodgson

I must try to pay you a visit, if I am ever again in England.

A British newspaper, the *Gazette*, dated November 1889, ran the following account headed 'A Desolate Spot':

The Island of Tristan d'Acunha, in the South Atlantic, was recently visited by Captain Fearon, of the ship *Dawpool*. In a letter sent to his friends at Cockermouth, he gives an interesting account of what he saw. The island is only six miles across, and with the exception of a small portion is uninhabitable. On that patch some 80 people, descendants of English soldiers from the Cape of Good Hope and a few negro women who were afterwards imported, eke out an existence, although they are often without some of the necessaries of

---

48 Caroline's grandmother. She often visited the Chestnuts to see the family, both as a child with her parents and later with her sisters or cousins to help 'entertain' her aunts and Uncle Edwin.

life. When the inhabitants saw Captain Fearon's ship lying off the island, some of them went to it in small boats. They had some vegetables with them, which they eagerly bartered for flour, tea, coffee, and sugar. One of the men in the boats was a venerable grey-beard, a native of Holland, aged 82. He was wrecked on the island 52 years ago, and has remained there ever since. Captain Fearon was surprised to find on the island the Rev. E. H. Dodgson, of the Chestnuts, Guildford, Surrey. He has been there for eight years, ministering to the inhabitants of this lonely island without fee or reward. The inhabitants are discontented, and expressed to the Captain a hope that the British Government would remove them to a more favoured region. They said all the Government aid for them was to send a man-of-war once a year, and this was their only communication with the outer world.

In November 1889, Charles received a letter from Rev. William Arthur Purey-Cust (1855–1938), son of the dean of York and rector of Belton near Grantham, who showed a great interest in Tristan da Cunha. Charles replied on 11 December (MS: Jon Lindseth Collection):

Dear Mr. Cust,

I fear you will have thought me very neglectful in leaving so long unnoticed the interesting letter I received from you on Nov. 22nd, about my brother and his work at Tristan d'Acunha. But I forwarded it, the same day, to my sisters at Guildford, who are far more able than I am to give you the information you desire, as my brother has long observed the rule of sending each of them in turn a long letter, half-letter-half-journal, which has often been concocting for weeks, till at last a passing vessel carries off all the letters then ready to go. One of my sisters copies out portions of these letters, as a sort of budget to circulate among friends. They have been waiting for the return of some of this budget from its rounds, and in the course of a few days they will send it to you. Will you kindly, when you have read it, send it back to 'Miss Dodgson, The Chestnuts, Guildford'.

I am sure they would be glad that you should quote from the papers sent you, in any Diocesan Magazine or other periodical.

Also if you ever cared to write (specially if you gave some *Church* news) to 'Rev. E. H. Dodgson, Tristan d'Acunha, c/o Commissariat Officer, S. Helena', you would do a real kindness, and help to cheer his lonely life. Believe me

Very truly yours,

C. L. Dodgson

Edwin's health had deteriorated so much that the doctor on board HMS *Curaçoa*, visiting Tristan in December 1889, advised him, on medical grounds and as he was now unable to perform his duties on the island, that he should leave Tristan. He was granted passage to the Cape, together with nine other islanders, including six children. His departure from Tristan da Cunha was much to the dismay of the remaining islanders, there now being only sixty-four inhabitants. His influence on them had been profound, and he was long remembered as a friend who devoted eight years of his life to tending to their spiritual, moral and practical needs. Tristan was to be without a priest in charge for the next sixteen years.

Edwin wrote a personal memoir of his time on the island of Tristan da Cunha, kept with other personal papers by the descendants of the Dodgson family. This extract comes from that account:

The way in which it came about that I went to this outlandish place was rather curious. An uncle of mine saw in a newspaper a letter from a Chaplain of a Man-of-War saying how anxious the people were to have a clergyman who would also act as a school-master. My uncle cut out this letter and sent it to me, saying in a joke, 'Here is the very place for you to go to.' He was much horrified when I made up my mind to go there.

I should like to correct two false impressions which are very commonly held about the Tristanites. The first is that they have their property (cattle, sheep, etc.) in common. This is the exact opposite of the truth; I never knew any people more tenacious of their personal belongings: every family has its own mark, and the cattle and sheep are each of them marked soon after their birth, and even, when any of the people go away, they always leave their belongings in the charge of someone, except what they give away. The other common mistake is that the Tristanites are teetotallers. This is by no means the case.

I remember one man from the Cape came to live at Tristan in the hope that he might improve. I once asked his wife whether he had improved and she said he was much better, that instead of getting drunk every day, as he used to do at the Cape, he now only got drunk whenever he had the chance.

Tristan is now over-run with rats. We tried to keep these pests down with cats, but unfortunately the cats preferred chickens to rats . . .

Charles noted in his diary for 13 January 1890:

Sudden news arrived that Edwin has been ordered home, by a doctor, and will be at Guildford in a few days.

Charles wrote to Edwin from Oxford on 18 January 1890 (MS: Berol Collection), having heard from his nephew, Stuart Dodgson Collingwood, about Edwin's condition:

My dear Edwin,

Let me join, with my pen, the chorus of voices who will have bidden you welcome. I was very glad to learn from Stuart that you had arrived in sufficiently good case *not* to have to take to your bed. More about you he did not know: I daresay I shall be hearing from you yourself, ere long, more details of your condition. I must manage to come over for a day, soon, to see you, as I fear you will hardly be up to paying me a visit *here*, as yet.

While I think of it, I'll mention a few people, to whom your return to England ought to be notified: though quite possibly you have written to all of them already.

(1) Bishop of St. Helena.

(2) Secretary of S.P.G.

(3) Publisher of the *Guardian* (that they may cease sending you copies of that paper).

(4) Rev. E. F. C. Noott, Magdalen College, Oxford (he asks after you, with the deepest interest, whenever we meet).

(5) Rev. W. A. Purey-Cust, Belton Rectory, Grantham (an old Christ Church man, takes deep interest in Tristan, would much like getting a few lines from *you*, I'm sure).

(6) Rev. H. Walmisley, Iffley Vicarage, Oxford (I have introduced myself to them, as *your* brother, as perhaps I may have told you before) . . .

Always your affectionate brother,
C.L.D.

In time, Edwin recovered, and after nearly a year he seemed anxious to get back to the South Atlantic, although he never returned to Tristan da Cunha.

The Dodgson family maintained a link with Tristan da Cunha, sending gifts from time to time, and corresponding with the islanders and the various clergymen who succeeded Edwin. Louisa, in particular, kept up a correspondence with some of the islanders who had sought a new life in America.

This is an extract from a letter written by Cornelia Beetham to Louisa, dated 21 June 1890 (MS: Amy Irene Jaques Collection). Cornelia had left Tristan around the same time as Edwin.

Dear Miss Dodgson,
I take my pen in hand to write you these few lines hoping to find you well as it leaves me at present. I received your letters and was very glad to hear from you. We are all getting on pretty well. I like America a good deal better than the Island. Please let me know when the next Man-of-War is going to the Island.

I have been Confirmed. Please let your Brother know this. All the family send him kind regards – to you all also . . .

Louisa continued her correspondence for the rest of her life. One correspondent had remained on the island and reported the conditions on Tristan. Frances Repetto wrote on 7 April 1918 (MS: Amy Irene Jaques Collection), not knowing that Edwin had died earlier that year:

Dear Madam,

Once again I am writing to thank you for your kind letter which I received on the 23rd of November 1916, and [I] sent you one on the 16th of September by a French ship. I had to wait nearly 13 months. Tristan seems such an out of the way place. There are a hundred and eight inhabitants at Tristan. I do hope someday a clergyman may come to live amongst us to teach us more. I often think of your dear brother when he was at Tristan. I send him many thanks for if it was not for him I would not be what I am today. His kindness I shall never forget and it makes me feel very sorry to know that he is now very feeble. May we all meet in that bright home above, never to part again. If he is alive, please tell him that I thank him very much for all he did in helping me to get on. I am a Widow now with 7 children, three daughters and 4 sons. My eldest daughter is married and has two little girls. We saw eight ships this summer and got five; the last one, a steamer, on the 30th of March ... I have an aunt 88 years old and very smart for her age. Your Brother will know her by name, Miss Cotton, because he stayed with her when at Tristan. Also she gave up the house to Mr. Barrow when he was at Tristan. I do hope this letter will find you all well and that I shall hear from you again. I often think of my friends so far away and pray for them ... We have no church at Tristan and it feels very lonesome on Sundays. I keep Sunday School for my own children and for any others who wish to come, but I am very sorry to say there's very few. With all kind wishes from myself and family, believe me

Your sincere friend,

Frances C. Repetto

*Tristan islanders with their boat*

# Final Career

In October 1890 Edwin Dodgson was appointed by the SPG to go to the Cape Verde islands as clergyman at St Vincent, a post he held for some years. Charles wrote a letter dated 2 December 1890 to Gertrude Chataway (1866–1951), a long-time friend and correspondent, from which this extract is taken (MS: Berol Collection):

> In a former letter of yours, you said that your mother was interested in hearing about my brother who was then at Tristan d'Acunha: so perhaps she may care to hear (I may have told you some of this before) that he came back, ill, nearly a year ago: he is much better now, and has again gone abroad on clerical work – but not to the same place. This time the S.P.G. have sent him to St. Vincent's, which is the chief of the Cape Verde Islands. It is a great change for him. At Tristan he was 'monarch of all he surveyed', and could carry on matters ecclesiastical exactly as he liked – which was delightful for such an extreme 'Ritualist' as he is. But the Cape Verde Islands are *Portuguese* property: and the Church, established there, is *Roman*: so that he finds himself in the novel position (shared by a Baptist Minister, who also has a congregation there) of being regarded as a 'Nonconformist Minister'! Also he has no *church* at all, but has to officiate (for the handful of members of the English Church – chiefly telegraph-clerks – who reside there) in a *room* lent for the purpose. He has only been a few weeks there: my sisters at Guildford have had two letters from him, giving a very cheerful account of his new life, and the friendly reception he has had from all.

Edwin continued to write home from St Vincent to his siblings. This letter was sent to Louisa on 29 December 1891 (MS: Amy Irene Jaques Collection):

Dearest Loui,

Many thanks for your letter etc. and also to you and Maggie for the chess men and board which are very acceptable. First, as to your letter – I don't know why you thought that I shouldn't get it till long after Christmas. The mail leaves Southampton every 4th Thursday and arrives here on the following Saturday week at about 6 a.m. with the regularity of clockwork. Your letter accordingly left England with Maggie's and Eva's (the 'Italian steamer' is a myth) on the 18th inst. and got here at 6 a.m. on the 26th. If you happen to miss the *Thursday*, letters posted not later than the mid-day post on Saturday 'via Lisbon' will be sent overland to that place, and will *most probably* catch our mail there on Monday, but of course it is safest to post letters for this Island not later than early on the Thursday morning. If Earnest Wale told you that he had had a 'long letter' from me, I fear he said 'the thing which is not' – you can hardly call half a sheet a *long* letter. Surely I have told you about the Church long before this. It was finished in time to be used for Service on the 1st Sunday in October and, since then, it has been regularly in use both Sundays and weekdays. I have only begun a *weekday* evening Service a few weeks ago – on Friday evenings at 7.30 p.m. One Friday there were 2 people, and another time there were 3, but on all other occasions *nobody* has turned up. The Church *will* hold about 90 people. The average Sunday congregation averages about 25. I really don't think the Church wants any fittings at present as the St. Nicholas Missionary Society gave us a complete set of Altar linen etc. The only things now wanting are a pair of flower vases (about 8 inches high) fitted with 'bouquet holders' with tubes for the Altar. If you like to give them, they will be very acceptable, but if they are too expensive, I know you have plenty to do with your money, we can quite afford to buy them out of Church funds. I have not yet received the parcel from Wales, but I have received the chess and children's books and Altar linen from Mr. Green, for which many thanks. There are so few children here, who care for reading, that I think it would be hardly worth while at present for me to have any *more* books for their perusal. Many thanks for your offer. I think I *have* acknowledged everything I have got from Guildford. Maggie never enclosed any list of *un*acknowledged parcels – perhaps she found that there *were* none! Before I forget please get me from the stores a 15*s* 'Corridor lamp' for the Church with a supply of wicks etc. They had better send it direct to Cardiff to be forwarded here. I will send you the money for it as soon as I know the amount due. I was rather surprised the other day by a carpenter here. I had been to his house the day before to see his wife – they are dissenters – and I tried to shew her that the Chapel 'Love Feasts' were not the same as Holy Communion, and we then went on to talk of other things in quite a friendly way till I went away. Imagine my amazement when I met the husband next day, with whom I have always been very friendly, to find him almost incoherent with rage. He abused me like a pick-pocket. I couldn't make out why – and ended by telling me that if he had been at home the day before 'it would have been bad for me', and that I was never to enter his house again! I have always been particularly friendly with both of them and I have been in the habit of going to see them about once a fortnight. A short time ago, when I happened to be a little longer than usual between visits, the wife told me that 'I was quite a stranger'! I suppose there must be some misunderstanding somewhere, which I must try to set right. Another American gentleman here – a Baptist – came to see me the other day when I was seedy, and after about a 2 hour talk he left in quite a friendly way but saying that he could never come to Church again as I was so intolerant. My 'intolerance' consisted in saying that Dissenters couldn't be considered as *belonging* to the Church, while they repudiated his teaching etc. – but I was careful to add that it was not *my* business to judge of the *spiritual* state of any one – that only GOD could do that. I feel rather comforted by these occurrences, for if the Devil takes the trouble to try and hinder the work here, there must be some work going on which he is afraid of – don't you think so? It is rather dreary work having only these *indirect* evidences of spiritual work to feed upon, but I try to be patient and not let myself be disheartened. 'GOD's ways are not our ways.' I am rather laid up this week, and haven't been out of the house since Sunday, but I hope I shall be all right for next Sunday. Many thanks to Fanny and

Maggie for their photos: and also to Maggie for *Bedside Readings* which will be very useful. I don't much care for Drummond's new book, as far as I have read. It has rather a dissenterish flavour.

6/1/92 There were very good congregations on Sunday – particularly in the evening – but *no one* but myself at Holy Communion. The young man whom I was preparing for Holy Communion has left the Island with his mother after the death of his father who died from the effects of taking some spirits of salt in mistake for rum. I think I told you about him – it was a very sad case. The boy's mother was going to take her children back to her old home in England, where she knew the clergyman to whom I wrote at her request about George (my pupil) so I hope he [will] still carry on his preparation. I quite thought I had sent you the Lloyds' direction, but perhaps it is just as well that I didn't, for they have both been much worried by a great row there has been at the Telegraph Station, and Mr. Lloyd was ordered back here before his holidays were properly over. They know *your* direction, so they might easily have communicated with you if they had wished to do so. I daresay you will hear or see something of the Holloways before long. Captain Holloway was Manager of one of the coaling firms here for some years. They were very kind to me, and I was very intimate with them and taught the two boys regularly. They ... are very nice people, and I miss them very much. They are now settled in a house of their own near Bristol – Elmcôte, Sneyd Park, Clifton, Bristol is their address. I have just had the rare pleasure of slaying a mosquito which settled on my hand meaning to make a good supper under my very nose! This letter is of a more respectable length than any I have written lately. Please forward the enclosures to their respective destinations. If you ever yield to the temptation of putting a letter inside one of my parcels, you may have to pay a fine of about £40! But the postage by the mail has been reduced from *your* end to 2½ the ½ ounce though *I* have still to pay 80 reis (rather over 4*d*). Best love

Your very affectionate brother,

E. H. Dodgson

Sometimes the correspondence between Edwin and the rest of his family was disrupted by other circumstances – in this case an outbreak of cholera in England. Edwin was able to write but not receive letters, as this extract, dated around September 1892, illustrates (MS: Amy Irene Jaques Collection):

> The Congregations are wretchedly small this hot weather, and spiritual matters altogether look very black and stagnant. It is a great comfort to me that my Godsons are away from this most irreligious place. Most people have got colds now. They sit in draughts trying to keep cool and this is the result. Also prickly heat is very maddening just now. As for myself, my great wish is that I was a herd of cattle living in a field with a post in the middle. Have you again settled down at the Chestnuts? It is hard to believe that you have really been at Guildford for 24 years! By the bye, I quite forgot whether I asked you to send my carte[49] to my two Godsons – if not please get half a dozen from Walker, Regent Street, and send two to Ardingly, one to George Eveleigh, Pope Carr, Matlock Bank, near Derby, and send one to me here for a telegraph clerk. I enclose a cheque for general purposes and towards defraying my debt. I received a large parcel of boys' books a few weeks ago without any clue as to the donor. My only vestige of one is from the fact that soon after I came here I got a message from old Mr. Boggis through Mr. Green asking if I would like any boys' books. I thankfully accepted his offer, but as nothing seemed to come of it, it passed out of my mind. I wish you could make out about them, but a man can't expect to be thanked, if he doesn't send his name.
>
> 8/9/92 9.39 p.m. I have just heard that there will be a mail to England tomorrow morning, so I shall not be able to send the cheque till next Monday or Thursday by the Royal Mail – you can send me nothing for the present except letters and newspapers, for no passengers or parcels from England are allowed to land here because of the cholera – a Collier came in from Cardiff last night (or this morning) with nothing for me on board and now a telegram has

---

[49] Almost certainly he means a carte-de-visite, a photographic portrait.

been sent to Cardiff saying that nothing but coals will be allowed to be landed here for the present, so good bye to my chance of getting Psalters etc. for some time to come. We hear that the cholera has now appeared in Liverpool and London as well as at Gravesend. A terrier belonging to one of the people here came in the Collier and it had to be fumigated before it was allowed to land – I hope it liked it! I will send letters to Lizzie, Eva, Stuart, and Alfred Dymes next week. It strikes me that I am improving in epistolary duties. I believe I shall have a new man Communicant next Sunday. I was rather encouraged by hearing the other day that some words of disapproval of mine were discussed at dinner at the Telegraph Station with good results, so perhaps after all there may be some good leaven working in the hearts of some of the young fellows. A boy of 15 came out as a Clerk at the Telegraph Station about 5 weeks ago, and has never yet been to Church. It is very sad, but he is coming to play chess with me some night next week, so I hope to make friends with him by degrees. He seems a nice boy, but he naturally goes with the swim. I was dining with the Telegraph Manager the other day, and in talking afterwards I managed to get an opening for remonstrating with him for allowing their billiards table and tennis court to be used on Sunday. He didn't say much, but I think he felt rather uncomfortable. Best love

Your very affectionate brother,

E. H. Dodgson

Finally mail was allowed to be sent from home again. This letter, thanking his sister for her letters, was sent to sister Louisa on 13 December 1893 (MS: Amy Irene Jaques Collection):

Dearest Loui,

Many thanks for your 2 letters received within three days of each other, by the collier last Wednesday, and by the Royal Mail on Sunday. I am taking a holiday today, as I have a bad cold and a headache, so I feel half stupefied. The '82' problem is very neat – if you did not know that .5 recurring = 5/9, perhaps you are also unaware of the death of Queen Anne! And may you *really* multiply the numerator and denominator by 11, so as to make 5/9 into 55/99!

By the bye, I met with a problem the other day, which tickled me a good deal. 'If there were 100 ears of corn in a barn, and a rat wanted to have them all in its hole, how many times would it have to go into the barn, if it only could take away 3 ears at a time?' Of course the rat's hole was not *in* the barn. I heard from 'Tites' Synge from Dartmoor last Sunday – he says 'I asked the Chaplain, if he would like to exchange with you, but he didn't seem to jump at it' – he knows how much I should like to be a gaol Chaplain. Many thanks to you and Maggie for the motto cards, only I should like to alter St. Paul's words into 'Whose I am, and Whom *I try* to serve', for, as far as *I* can see, my actual work for Him is infinitesimally small. I have to struggle against a sort of Gallio acquiescence in the irreligious state of things here – it is so hard to preserve the happy medium of feeling – I mean to keep up being sorry for the people without being depressed and disheartened one's self.

I have just lost one of my boy pupils – Earnest Saffery. Mr. S. with his wife and children have just gone to one of the other Islands to superintend the Telegraph Station there. I am very sorry to lose them, as I like them all very much. They are Irvingites,[50] but come regularly to Church and Mrs. S. to the Holy Communion and Mr. S. has been playing regularly at the Children's Service, but I think I have secured a successor. I have heard Canon Mason several times at St. Nicholas, and I liked his sermons very much. I fancy these clever men have two styles of preaching. I once went to a Retreat conducted by Father Benson, and certainly his addresses and meditations were terribly deep, and his books are the same, but his parochial sermons are delightfully simple. It must seem queer to him to be now merely one of the Cowley Brethren after so long being the Superior of the Community, and to have one of his underlings – Father Page

---

50   Irvingites follow the doctrine of the Scottish divine Edward Irving (1792–1834), minister of a church in Caledonian Road from 1822 and later Regent Square, London. He was a popular preacher who believed in the nearness of the 'second coming'. He was found guilty of heresy and deprived of his ministerial status. He helped set up the Catholic Apostolic Church, its members being called Irvingites.

– over him![51] I am very glad to hear that the coal strike is really at an end at last, but I fear that it has – and *will* for some time to come – caused terrible distress among the poor – for depend upon it the masters will keep up the price of coal as much as they can. There are at least *2* more colliers due here from Cardiff before Christmas Day.[52] I hope they will bring something for me! Now for my usual question – I wonder how soon I shall get it answered in the affirmation. *Has anyone sent 6d in stamps to the E.C.U.?* Many thanks for *Dr. Pusey's Life*, when it comes. I have seen several notices of it in the *Church Times*, and I certainly *long* to read it, but I fear it is terribly expensive. However, it will be a sort of family treasure, when it gets back to Guildford.

Best love and wishes for the new year,

Your very affectionate brother,

E. H. Dodgson

Another letter was sent to his brother Skeffington, dated 27 April 1895 (MS: Amy Irene Jaques Collection). Skeffington had just been appointed vicar of Vowchurch, Herefordshire:

Dear Skeff,

I have just heard that you have had a living given to you. I'm sure it must be a great relief to you to exchange an uncertain stipend as Curate for a permanent one – as far as your life in *this* world is concerned – though of course it will involve a good deal more responsibility. May GOD grant that you may be equal to it! I hear occasionally of you and yours from the Guildford party, but I always

---

51    The Cowley Fathers, or the Society of St John the Evangelist, is a religious community of men in the Church of England founded in Oxford in 1866 by Richard Meux Benson (1824–1915), who was at that time vicar of Cowley, a Christ Church living. They described themselves as a congregation of mission priests. Benson was formerly a student at Christ Church, and was photographed by Dodgson.

52    Miners' wages were lowered as the price of coal dropped; the mine owners were keen to make the same profit if not increase their profits. The miners elected to call a strike in 1893. The owners brought in miners from elsewhere and locked out the striking miners until they accepted reduced pay. Violence broke out and police were brought in to guard the collieries.

take for granted that no news is good news. The last thing I heard about you was that you had changed your lodgings for the better, so as to get 2 sitting rooms instead of only one. I hope Isa and all your bairns are flourishing. There is rather an excitement here just now, as Jabez Balfour, the 'Liberator' director has at last been given up by the Argentine Government – having come to the end of his pecuniary resources – and is expected to arrive here at any moment in the *Tartan Prince* en route for England.[53] One gentleman here told me today that he would like just to see Balfour, so that he might be able to say that he had seen the 'biggest blackguard in the world'! I see from the newspapers that the Government majority is dwindling down, and I should think there *must* soon be a dissolution, and then good bye to the Home Rulers. I suppose the liberal unionists will have a turn.

Now with best love to Isa, yourself, and your youngsters – especially my God-daughter Zoe Frances – I remain

Your very affectionate brother,

E. H. Dodgson

On 29 July 1895, Charles recorded in his diary:

Heard, from Loui, that Edwin has at last made up his mind to give up foreign work, and settle in England, and that he expects to arrive about August the 2nd. He had told me some time ago that he wishes to get appointed Chaplain to a Prison.

Charles used another of his social connections to assist in this proposal, writing to Sir Michael Hicks Beach, Chancellor of the Exchequer, for help in obtaining such a position for Edwin. However, there had been a misunderstanding, and Edwin no longer sought a position in the prison service.

---

[53]  Jabez Balfour, MP, set up the Liberator Building Society. Instead of advancing money to home buyers, the Liberator advanced money to buy, at a high price, properties owned by Balfour. Once the swindle was discovered Balfour fled to Argentina, where he was eventually captured and sent home on a ship. He was sentenced to fourteen years in prison.

After Edwin had again convalesced at the Dodgson home in Guildford, Charles wrote to Lord Salisbury (MS: Hatfield) in the hopes of finding him a suitable post in England. The letter, written from Eastbourne without Edwin's knowledge, is dated 17 September 1895.

Dear Lord Salisbury,

Many thanks for your letter … There is another matter – more of a personal one – which I will venture to put before you.

To put the gist of it in a few words, it is that I request you to bear in mind the name of my brother, the Rev. Edwin Heron Dodgson, in case you should ever be disposed to think him a fit man for some clerical post which may be in your gift.

He has now been some 25 years in Holy Orders. After several years of work in England, he acted on what he believed to be a distinct 'call', in undertaking the charge of the island of Tristan d'Acunha. In that place of utter banishment from society he worked, single-handed, for some 7 or 8 years. After that he worked for some years in Zanzibar, having the charge of a large school of boys captured from the slavers [Charles has the dates muddled here]. It was only when the doctors pronounced that he would certainly die of ague if he stayed there, that he gave up Zanzibar. For the last few years he has been in the Cape Verde Islands, being the English Clergyman sent by the S.P.G. to St. Vincent. Altogether he has been about 20 years abroad: and he is now back in England, where he would be glad to get regular work to settle down to. After working single-handed for so many years, I doubt if he would find a *curacy* at all workable. A small living, sufficient for a bachelor (I don't believe he will ever marry), would be the ideal home for him. Anything *I* say, as to his qualifications, must of course be weakened by the fact of my being his brother. Still I will venture to say that I think it would be hard to find any clergyman more *thoroughly* devoted to the work of a priest. His views are High Church: to *me* they seem rather extreme: still there are many posts where such views are almost essential for the harmony of the place, and where to present a marked Evangelical would be to inflict a real calamity on the parish. His power of winning the affection of boys and young men seems to be almost unique: and *they*, I fancy, are often the hardest to deal with of all. I will only add that neither he, nor anybody else, has any idea that I am mentioning this to you. Believe me

Sincerely yours,

C. L. Dodgson

Nothing came of this plea. Once Edwin had recovered from his illness, he yearned to get back, yet again, to the South Atlantic. He was appointed vicar of Jamestown, St Helena, in 1896, and he held this post until 1898. In a letter to his brother Skeffington, dated 30 October 1896, written from St James' Vicarage, St Helena, he adds a postscript:

I am very busy – very well and very happy. This place suits me exactly in every way.

While Edwin was at Jamestown, his brother Charles died at Guildford on 14 January 1898. He was buried in the Mount Cemetery, on the hillside overlooking the Dodgson family home at the Chestnuts. The family passed the news to Edwin. Writing briefly to Skeffington on 8 February

*Jamestown, St. Helena*

1898, Edwin asked about a wooden flute he wanted to acquire as a gift for one of his parishioners.

> Please send me one of the 1/6 flutes you mentioned, and get the money from Wilfred out of my share of Charles' property. This is the first gap in our family circle – who will make the next?

# Retirement

Edwin returned again to Guildford in 1898. He wrote to the SPG that year saying that he 'did not feel equal to much locomotion' as his back and legs had been weakened by the ague he had suffered in Zanzibar, but he was willing to go back to Tristan. The SPG decided against any further postings abroad.

In 1901, a doctor pronounced that Edwin had damaged his spinal cord as a result of the fall on a ship when returning from Tristan. Edwin gradually became more and more disabled. He retired from clerical duties, spending some years at St Barnabas' Homes from 1904 until 1912. He then returned to live out the rest of his life with his sisters at Guildford.

Edwin died on 3 January 1918. The funeral took place on 7 January at St Nicholas, Guildford, his place of worship during his retirement years, although his ability to walk had deteriorated to such an extent that he was visited by priests at home in the last few months. He was also buried in the Mount Cemetery, Guildford. An obituary appeared in the *Surrey Advertiser* dated Saturday 14 January under the heading 'Death of the Rev. E. H. Dodgson, Brother of "Lewis Carroll", Noble Work on a Lonely Island', which stated:

> The funeral took place at Guildford Cemetery on Monday of the Rev. Edwin Heron Dodgson, who died at The Chestnuts, Guildford, on the previous Thursday at the age of 71 years. He was the youngest son of the Ven. Archdeacon Dodgson, of Croft Rectory, Yorkshire, and a brother of 'Lewis Carroll' (the Rev. C. L. Dodgson), author of 'Alice in Wonderland'.
>
> Mr. Dodgson had a romantic and adventurous career as a missionary. After holding curacies in England, in 1879 he became principal of Kiungani School, Zanzibar. About a year later a friend of

his saw in the papers an appeal for the ministrations of a missionary on the lonely little island in the South Atlantic known as Tristan da Cunha. He showed it to Mr. Dodgson, and the latter was inspired by the call and straightway set sail for the island, which is extremely difficult to access. The coast line is so precipitous and the weather so consistently stormy that landing is well nigh impossible, and the only spot at which this can be undertaken is swept unceasingly by the Atlantic breakers. How lonely and desolate a spot it is will be gathered from the fact, vouched for by Miss Dodgson, that only a few months ago the first mail for 12 years reached England from the island, and with it was a letter from Mr. Dodgson's congregation there, which was a source of great comfort to him in his declining years . . .

The Dodgson family received a number of letters from the people of Tristan da Cunha on Edwin's death. The following letter, dated 12 May 1918, was written by one of Edwin's former pupils on the island (MS: Amy Irene Jaques Collection). It has been edited for spelling and grammar.

We were all so very sorry to hear of the Rev. Dodgson's death. He was always so good and kind to everyone. I hope that he did not have much pain. He was not a very strong person and the work was too much for him. The people on our island have not forgotten him. We must also thank you very much for your kindness to us all. They [presumably some gifts] have come in most useful to us. I was one of Rev. Dodgson's pupils. Wishing you every happiness and God's blessing from all on the island. I do wish and pray to the Good God that the world will be in peace next time you write, as I hope that you will drop us a line next time the mail comes. From
Mr. Tom Rogers

Some years after Edwin's death, his sister Louisa arranged for a memorial to be sent to Tristan da Cunha, to be placed in the church. The inscription on the brass memorial tablet, which was sent in 1927, read:

IN LOVING MEMORY OF
THE REV. EDWIN HERON DODGSON
MISSIONARY PRIEST-IN-CHARGE
OF TRISTAN DA CUNHA
1880–1884 AND 1886–1889
'LOOKING UNTO JESUS.'

The vicar on Tristan at the time, Rev. R Pooley, wrote back to Louisa to thank her for the memorial:

Tristan Da Cunha
Easter 1927

Dear Miss Dodgson,
　　Many thanks for the brass tablet in memory of the late Rev. Dodgson. We shall unveil two tablets on Sunday May 15th – the Rev. H. Rogers' (who died May 14) [Henry Martyn Rogers] and the other one – yours.
　　Quite a number of people remember the Rev. Dodgson, to whom they owe their knowledge of the three R's.
　　Excuse more. I have many letters to write.
　　Yours truly,
　　R. Pooley

May God's richest blessing rest upon you and your work, whatever it be, in your advancing years. As the body grows weaker, may faith become stronger.

# Postscript

---

In 1961, the volcano on Tristan da Cunha erupted, and the people were evacuated to the United Kingdom. Although much damage was done to the cultivated plateau, many of the islanders elected to return once the volcano had become dormant again.

In 1981, the island of Tristan da Cunha issued three postage stamps commemorating Edwin Dodgson's arrival in 1881; 10p shows a youthful Edwin in England, 20p shows Edwin with the island in the background, and 30p shows Edwin teaching a group of islanders. A mini-sheet depicts the Dodgson family at Croft-on-Tees.

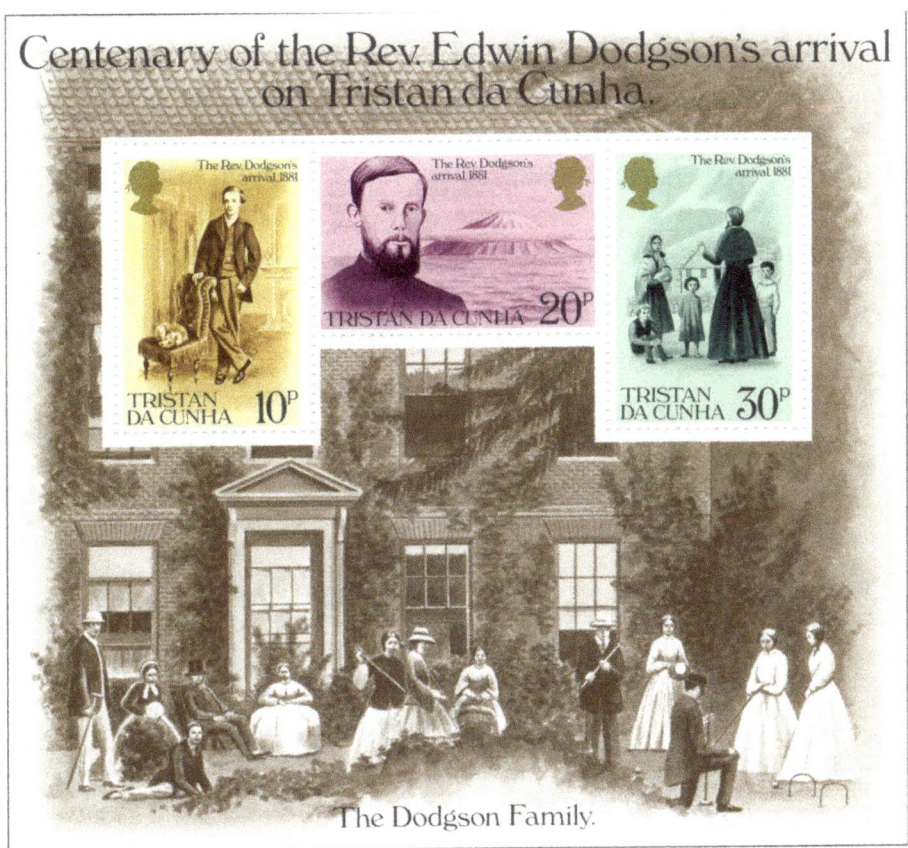

Our two main sources of information have been *Tristan da Cunha 1506–1902* by J Brander, 1940 (from which we have quoted material in the archives of the British Admiralty and the Colonial Office), and *Churches of the South Atlantic Islands* by Edward Cannan, 1992 (containing material from the SPG archives). Extracts from entries in Charles L Dodgson's diaries are published here by kind permission of the trustees of the Charles L Dodgson Estate. Extracts from letters are published by kind permission of the Amy Irene Jaques Collection.

# Chronology of Edwin Dodgson's Life

---

| 1846 | 30 June: born at the Rectory, Croft-on-Tees, the youngest of eleven children |
|------|------|
| 1851 | Mother dies when he is four and a half years old |
| 1856–60 | Attends small private school at North Stainley |
| 1858–60 | Attends Twyford School near Winchester |
| 1860–64 | Attends Rugby School |
| 1868 | Edwin's father dies at home and Edwin's brother Charles moves the family to the Chestnuts, Guildford |
| 1868 | Passes examination for the civil service |
| 1869–71 | Considers various career opportunities and finally decides to train for the ministry at Chichester Theological College |
| 1873 | Ordained deacon |
| 1874 | Ordained priest |
| 1874–75 | Curate at Odd Rode, Cheshire |
| 1875–77 | Curate at Helmsley, Yorkshire |
| 1877–79 | Curate at All Saints, Shrewsbury, Shropshire |
| 1879 | Principal of Kiungani School, Zanzibar, under Bishop Edward Steere of the Central African Mission, arriving in April but sent home in November as a result of poor health |
| 1880 | Becomes missionary for the SPG |
| 1881 | Embarks for Tristan da Cunha via St Helena on 8 January, being appointed priest in charge and school teacher on behalf of the SPG. Arrives 25 February 1881 |

| | |
|---|---|
| 1884 | At the end of the year, he returns to England, but he suffers a bad fall down an open hatchway on board en route and requires medical attention on arrival home |
| 1885 | In November, fifteen of the men on Tristan tragically killed when their lifeboat capsizes |
| 1886 | Edwin returns to Tristan da Cunha as a result of this tragedy |
| 1889 | In December, ordered home on grounds of ill health resulting from the previous bad fall and depression |
| 1890 | Arrives home in January. In October, appointed chaplain at St Vincent on Cape Verde islands |
| 1895 | Returns home as a result of poor health and mobility problems |
| 1896–98 | Appointed vicar of Jamestown, St Helena |
| 1898 | Struggling with ever-decreasing mobility, returns home to Guildford |
| 1904–12 | Severely disabled, spends periods of respite at home and at St Barnabas, East Grinstead, a home for retired clergy |
| 1912–18 | Nursed at home by his sisters |
| 1918 | Dies at the Chestnuts on 3 January and is buried at the Mount Cemetery, Guildford |

# Further Reading

Anne Clark Amor (ed.). *Letters to Skeffington Dodgson from his Father.* White Stone Publishing, The Lewis Carroll Society, 1990.

David Lansley. *Wilfred Dodgson of Shropshire, Land Agent and Brother of Lewis Carroll*, by David Lansley. White Stone Publishing, The Lewis Carroll Society, 2011. ISBN: 987-0-904117-36-3

Edward Wakeling. *Skeffington Hume Dodgson, Brother of Lewis Carroll, Vicar of Vowchurch.* Privately published, 1992. Available from the author at edward.wakeling@btinternet.com

*Skeffington Hume Dodgson*

*Wilfred Dodgson*

# Index